Everyday Soul

Everyday Soul

Awakening the Spirit in Daily Life

BRADFORD KEENEY, PH.D.

RIVERHEAD BOOKS
New York

Riverhead Books
Published by The Berkley Publishing Group
A member of Penguin Putnam Inc.
200 Madison Avenue
New York, New York 10016

Excerpt from "Love Dogs" is from *The Essential Rumi*, translated by
Coleman Barks. Reprinted by permission of Maypop Books.

Copyright © 1996 by Bradford Keeney, Ph.D.
Book design by Jaime Robels
Cover design by Lisa Amoroso
Cover photograph © 1996 by Howard Bjornson/Photonica
Front-cover photograph of the author © 1996 by Noel Sutherland

First Riverhead hardcover edition: October 1996
First Riverhead trade paperback edition: December 1997
Riverhead trade paperback ISBN: 1-57322-634-3

The Putnam Berkley World Wide Web site address is
http://www.berkley.com

The Library of Congress has catalogued the Riverhead hardcover edition
as follows:

Keeney, Bradford P.
Everyday soul: awakening the spirit in daily life / Bradford Keeney.
p.   cm.
ISBN 1-57322-044-2 (alk. paper)
1. Spiritual life.   I. Title.
BL624.K46   1996   96-22519   CIP
291.4'4—dc20

Printed in the United States of America
10   9   8   7   6   5   4   3   2   1

To Ikuko Osumi, Sen-sei

♪ This little light of mine, I'm gonna let it shine,
  Oh, this little light of mine, I'm gonna let it shine,
  Oh, this little light of mine, I'm gonna let it shine,
  Let it shine, let it shine, let it shine.

—TRADITIONAL GOSPEL SONG

Contents

ACKNOWLEDGMENTS

I want to thank all of the elders, spiritual teachers, shamans, and traditional healers who have guided me in the matters of spirit. In particular, I am deeply grateful to Ikuko Osumi, Sen-sei, one of the last living masters of the Japanese art of seiki-jutsu, who has devotedly nurtured and cared for my family.

I wish to express heartfelt acknowledgment for the inspiration and graceful management of this project by my literary agent, Arielle Eckstut, of James Levine Communications. In addition, I am indebted to Amy Hertz, senior editor of Riverhead Books, for her encouragement, guidance, and wisdom, and to the Nancy Connor Foundation for its support of my ongoing work.

I am especially grateful for the permission and blessing of my parents to write about our family story. And finally, love and affectionate appreciation to my wife, Marian, and my son, Scott. In the life of our home, I continue to find the everyday heart of spiritual truth.

Introduction

We must remember that the heart of our religions is alive and that each person has the ability within to awaken and walk in a sacred manner. The manner with which we walk through life is each man's most important responsibility and we should remember this with every new sunrise.

—THOMAS YELLOW TAIL

IGUASSU FALLS IS one of the geophysical hearts of our earth, forever pushing vital fluid into its South American river veins. Two hundred seventy-five cascades, as if representing the different countries of the world, form a mile-and-a-half-long crescent, with thunderous torrents of water plunging to a basin in cataracts more than two hundred feet high. Each day the water that crashes over the cliffs gives birth to an endless array of blue-sky rainbows. In the multicolored mist of these waterfalls, earth and sky are wed, reflecting the truth of life's mysterious relatedness.

Iguassu Falls is surrounded by a rich tropical rainforest that is home to innumerable plant varieties and innumerable species of birds, reptiles, insects, and mammals, including jaguars and mountain lions. Deep in this mass of matted vegetation live its ancient custodians, the Guaraní Indians. As a university professor and teacher of psychotherapy, I never imagined I would someday find myself in the midst of this rainforest culture praying with their spiritual elders.

I was brought to the heart of the South American rainforest in the same mysterious way I had been led all over the world, from the Kalahari Desert of southern Africa to the remote outback of Western Australia to the dense cities of Japan: through dreams. And now that I was sleeping under the canopy of the rainforest, I dreamed again. In the dream I saw the face of the revered Guaraní shaman, "the priest of the forest," looking at me though a ring of fire. Then I heard him make a loud, guttural sound, which woke me up. I opened my eyes and saw that he had in reality made a fire and was looking at me through it. He laughed and said, "I can also dream you."

The world of spirit not only teaches us how to enter the reality of dream, but inspires us to dream realities that nurture and bring forth the deepest qualities of our soul. The Andean shamans speak of a five-hundred-year-old prophecy that defines our present time as a second awakening of the Sacred Fire, a rekindling of the light within our hearts. Similarly, I have met spiritual people around the world who carry this fire and use it to help light the inner realms of others. This sacred light is spreading from one heart to another, moving itself without regard to color, belief, or nationality.

This gift of spirit is available to everyone, even those who are skeptical. I was brought into the heart of the spiritual mystery in spite of my efforts to avoid it. As an academic psychotherapist who had written numerous professional books, I was not eager to threaten the respectability of my career by seeking a public relationship with any shaman, traditional healer, medicine person, or spiritual elder.

It was the integrity and beauty of the spiritual life of indigenous people, not the promise of a miracle, power, or secret wisdom, that opened my heart. Spirit touches and moves our lives through the mystery of love and relationship. Holding both ecstasy and suffering, a spirited soul embraces all the longings of the heart. As Rumi poetically captures this:

Listen to the moan of a dog for its master.
That whining is the connection.

There are love dogs
no one knows the names of.

Give your life
to be one of them.

All spiritual traditions attune themselves to the heart's longing for the divine. Like the "love dogs" who moan for their master, they align themselves to receive grace through a heart that cries for divine presence. To spiritual seekers who give up asking for the divine because they think they haven't heard anything back, Rumi responds: "This longing you express is the return message."

Whether you're a regular churchgoer, a member of a synagogue, a meditator, a seeker wondering about finding a spiritual path, or someone who simply feels lost, this book is a guide for experiencing the divine in everyday life. In an ecumenical environment that draws upon the resources of diverse spiritual traditions, you are invited to discover your own connection to the Divine Spirit. Through personal anecdotes, practical exercises, and stories about various spiritual elders, the benefits of a spiritual life are made more accessible to you. Here you may initiate each day with the promise of valuable teachings and blessings.

Before you go on, pause to ask yourself what your present beliefs and assumptions are about spirituality. A spiritual life is more than a Sunday-morning affair, a bedtime prayer, a morning mantra, a weekend in a Native American sweat lodge, or a once-a-day meditation. Set aside whatever you have been told by someone else about the nature of the divine and consider what particular spirit or deity or sacred idea you most fully trust and are comfortable with. Whom would you cry out to if you were in an airplane that was suddenly diving toward the ground?

Hold yourself open to the possibility that you are aware of the presence of the sacred, whether in a beautiful work of art or in love. Your life already has been graced by spirited moments, regardless of whether they were consciously articulated as such. The birth of your child; falling in love; being moved by music, poetry, or dance; watching a morning sunrise—all are occasions of the divine. Begin your entry into everyday soul with the affirmation that the sacred, the spirit, the Divine Light, is already alive in your world. Our task is to awaken you more fully to its spirited presence in everyday life.

Throughout history, countless saints, healers, shamans, and mystics have learned how to breathe soul into the everyday. Filled with love and compassion, they have deeply enriched the lives of others. The entry into this spiritually blessed way of living begins with opening your heart and feeling the passion for soulful communion. A palpable experience of the divine does more than bring faith. It awakens an inner light that shows us how to move forward with a profound acceptance, deep knowing, and attuned sensitivity to the sacred essence pervading all of life. The center of the spiritual universe has already opened its heart to accept each of us. It is we who must say yes to the opening, and fall into the beauty and grace that await.

Everyday Soul

1 ♣ *Preparing the Ground*

☙

CHAPTER ONE

The Unquenchable Thirst

What you look for has come, but you do not know it.
—THE GOSPEL OF ST. THOMAS

WE ALL STOOD quietly in the garage, looking out at the hammering rain. It hadn't stopped pouring for seven days and nights, and no end was in sight. I was twelve years old and was beginning to wonder whether the world could actually be washed away. This was not ordinary rain. It was so thick you couldn't see through it, and it was loud enough to absorb all conversation. The downpour brought on a flood that the army corps of engineers said was not supposed to happen for another five hundred years. A similarly improbable flood had taken place the year before.

The community of Smithville, Missouri, was accustomed to seasonal flooding, but not like this. The whole town was covered with water, and the effort to sandbag the river banks had proven futile. As we waited without electricity, food, and drinking water, I felt a mythological appreciation for how nature was fully in charge of running the show and that all of our efforts to control life had made us blind to the fragile place we occupy. I prayed that the rain would stop and that baseball, candy, and soda pop would return to our small town.

When the rain began to let up, our worries quickly turned to speculating on what possibly could be left in the remains. We survived that flood, and our community's perseverance to survive helped my father, the town pastor, to persuade the congressmen in Washington, D.C., to build a dam. Years later, the floods that had tempted us to move somewhere else provided rich material for tall tales and helped turn a washed-out town into a booming summer lake resort.

I grew up watching floods come and go not only in the yearly thunderstorms but in the daily lives of the townspeople. They brought the floods and storms of their emotional lives to my father as they did to my grandfather, both of whom were Baptist preachers. There were no psychotherapists or counselors. People took their troubles to the preacher.

When the great flood nearly destroyed the whole town, the local people turned to my father for an answer. How could this happen and how were they to move forward with their lives? I remember how they all came to church the Sunday following the end of the rain, wondering what my father would say. The stench of flood was everywhere and piles of debris littered the streets. What hope could be resurrected from this calamity?

The answer came from the church itself. My father simply acknowledged that although everything seemed to be destroyed, a small miracle had taken place in the midst of the destruction. The altar table holding the church Bible had floated up to the ceiling and kept the Bible dry. It was the only thing in the church untouched by the muddy flood water. He didn't have to say anything else. It was not necessary to talk about psychological trauma, or emotional paralysis and the devastation of losing their homes in the flood. The explanations of psychology gave way to an experience of the sacred. People opened themselves to the image of that untouched Bible and it was enough to give them hope for the future. It was a light that shone through all the darkness that had fallen upon them.

In that moment, I learned how we move forward in times of trouble and distress by looking for the light that touches our soul and awakens our spirit. Floating above the practical realities of paying the bills, bandaging the cuts, and calming the emotions, we seek the spirit that breathes life and renewal into our being. I grew up seeing firsthand how spirituality can deeply touch and move people's lives, no matter how much ruin and destruction come upon them.

As a boy, I saw that behind the fear of climatic and emotional storms, people thirsted for more than shelter and security. They sought to be touched by a spiritual experience that would fill their hearts with ecstasy and healing. Our longing for spiritual experience is sometimes met with misfortune when our search goes awry and becomes trapped in an addiction. Addictions, whether to drugs, personal success, or intellectual understanding, mask the underlying search for spirit. They are misguided graspings for spiritual fulfillment and remind us that we are all in the same conundrum.

What is the Divine Light that quenches our spiritual thirst? It is the whole of your being, all of your heart and mind and body and sensory channels in its fullest encounter with all of creation. When you take on the whole creation with your whole being, you and that which is encountered become experienced as one. This temple of oneness is realized as Divine Light, the source from which you and all that you love are born and into which you will return. It is the vital force of life and the originating point for all creative expression.

♣ In my young adult years, after leaving the small farm town I had grown up in, my father retired from the country Baptist church and moved to a large midwestern city, where he co-pastored a Presbyterian city church. There the pastor was less a mediator of spirit and more a psychological counselor and attendant of Sunday ritual. Without the weekly stream of spirit into church and community life, my father turned to alcohol and began a fall into its habitual grip. Alcoholism, as a spiritual dis-ease, magnified his desire to escape the suffering of everyday life and provided a momentary glimpse of a bliss that the bottle managed to keep just out of reach. The plunge into drink took my father, as it has taken so many others, into the anguished truth of how desperate we are to quench our spiritual thirst. It destroyed his career as a pastor and took away most of his world. In the midst of his fall, I began my study of family therapy.

I brought my family into therapy, but to no avail. The stream of alcohol could not be stopped. It flooded our lives with despair and led to divorce, financial ruin, and threats of suicide. When my father hit every possible bottom short of death, the doctors were stunned by how he had managed to survive the amount of alcohol he was habitually consuming. He had become an improbable statistic akin to the only-once-every-five-hundred-years flood in the small town he had once helped save.

I eventually had to face the same realization that came over me as a boy when I stood gazing upon the torrential downpour that no one could imagine how to stop. The same uncontrollable force had entered our home life, and we were all silenced by our inability to stop its fall. It took many years for my father to find the "twelve steps" that would curb his fall into drink and move his life to professionally helping others who were burdened with emotional difficulties.

While I traveled throughout the world demonstrating how to work with troubled families, I not only couldn't help my father—I couldn't help the woman I lived with for many years. Our household was filled with hidden liquor bottles and an atmosphere charged with violence. I was not prepared to live with a problem drinker, even though I had grown up in an alcoholic family and was professionally trained to work with alcoholics. Over time, the tides of her drinking became higher and lower, until the definition of hitting bottom began to approach a life-threatening limit. In my case, the life that was threatened was my own. Under the influence, my companion tried to drive the car off the road and attacked me with a knife a number of times.

My home life worsened as my family therapy career was reaching its height. My books were required texts at family therapy graduate programs throughout the world, and I received a steady stream of invitations to lecture and teach others. I tried all the strategies and solutions of psychotherapy, but nothing worked. We tried moving to other cities. I studied our conversations for clues to unravel why our relationship was so unhealthy. I even tried getting drunk myself.

At the height of my career as a therapist, I paradoxically began realizing that psychology could not offer the help people needed in their deepest moments of suffering. It certainly hadn't helped me or my family. Its strategies for cure, though intelligent, were not rooted in what spiritual traditions have always known as the great healers: love and compassion. Psychological cures grew out of the intellect that saw mind and body as fixable mechanisms. Curing neuroses and psychological illness had taken the place of seeking spirit. And seeking spirit had become just another psychological abnormality. Psychology often misunderstands the shift to spirituality as denial or avoidance of the real world instead of seeing spirituality for what it really is: the ground on which all psychological drama is played out. A psychological explanation of a spiritual truth couldn't touch me in the same way I remembered being moved by the experience of spirit as a child. My profession had left its spiritual home.

I walked away from the narrowly defined limits of psychotherapy and began a spiritual pilgrimage to find help and renewal for my own life. I needed to have my hope reborn as it had been in my child-hood by the church Bible that hadn't been touched by the frightening flood waters.

During my desperation, a Native American spiritual teacher came to me and offered his traditional ways as a means of helping me re-connect to the spiritual truth I had known. Years before he heard me give a speech on ecological ways of understanding social interaction. After my talk, he approached me and said, "Our people not only know these things but have lived them for many years. Why don't you come learn from us how you can live what you are talking about?" At the time, I had no idea what he meant, but when my life hit bottom, I went to this man for help. In a prayer ceremony, he told me that something would take place in my life at the end of seven days that would change the course of my future. I had no idea what he was talking about, but I waited. On the end of that seventh day, my companion tried to stran-gle me. Something died within me at that moment and I was unable to fight her off. I was literally paralyzed with hopelessness. At the last moment, another pair of hands physically intervened and released her grip so that I was able to live.

The police and legal advisors urged me to press charges of assault, but my spiritual teacher suggested I turn to prayer for guidance. For someone whose whole career involved creating strategies and interven-tions for problem-solving, inactivity was almost too much to bear. But I remained still and watched my world systematically fall apart.

The deeper I dove into prayer, the more my thirst for ease and peace was quenched. I began meeting spiritual elders and healers from all around the world, who initiated me into a centered life suffused by a greater presence. I entered a life awakened by spirit.

The Addiction to Self

✠ To paraphrase William James, as soon as psychology became disinterested in mind, it became mindless. Similarly, its disinterest in soul resulted in its loss of soul. It is no surprise that after the psychologies of repair take care of our inner child, improve our communication, inflate our self-esteem, give us a better sex life, and illumine our gender identity, we are still left wanting something more.

It is ironic that the word "psychology" comes from the Greek, *psyche,* the beautiful maiden personifying the soul loved by Eros, the god of love. We have drifted far away from the meaning of psyche as a reference to spirit, vital life force, and soul. Today's psychology has succumbed to a hardened material view of human experience, explaining it in terms of neurochemical secretions and genetic hardware. It tempts us to see our life in terms of the performance of a concrete "self," something we assume is directing our everyday conduct, feelings, beliefs, and experiences, leading us to seek repair of our "self" whenever we feel distressed.

The psychological self I am speaking of is more popularly known to us as the "ego" or the "ego-centered self," held as the internal locus of our lives. When we overattend the emotional wounds of our ego, whether recognized as jealousy, anger, despair, loss of confidence, or deflated esteem, we trick ourselves into thinking that we are introducing more control over our lives. Our ego is happy with this control fix, but in the long run it adds to our suffering. We become excessively attenuated to preserving the status, prominence, and well-being of our ego at the cost of being less open to receiving the spiritual experiences that are capable of satisfying our deepest longings.

When we compare this psychological orientation of self-emphasis to the major spiritual traditions, we find a reversal. Throughout history, the world's most revered spiritual teachers have de-emphasized the importance of self and have invited us to see it as a fiction, an illusion, a distraction that easily gets us off course. Encountering others with love and compassion helps loosen the grip of emotional wounds. It doesn't bury them, short shrift them, or ignore them. Compassion is the great healer.

As we learn to experience others as though we were in their shoes, and as we help others, they in turn provide the ground for our own spiritual development. Without developing compassion, we cannot be free of the ego's emotional difficulties. Without other people, we cannot develop compassion. Those whom we often find the most challenging to our emotional well-being are often the ones who provide us with the opportunity to develop the firmest part of our spiritual being. That was certainly true of the woman I lived with. She taught me the first lesson of compassion: having enough compassion for myself to begin a spiritual journey.

Although many contemporary psychological explanations point to addiction as the basis for our suffering, they fail to recognize the underlying root addiction. On the surface it appears as an addiction to the importance of the ego, the never-ending confirmation of the existence and position of our inner self. However, I believe that the root addiction underneath this fixation on the self involves our desire to understand, the belief that we must make sense of life before we can know how to act in it. Without a steady diet of understanding, we fear we will have less control over influencing the outcomes of our lives. Psychology has become a principal agent in perpetuating this addiction of understanding.

The nature of human experience is far too complex to be explained by any psychological generalization. But the fact that we can't understand much doesn't mean that we should stop trying to fully participate in life. We continue to laugh even though we may have no idea why some things strike us as funny, and we continue to be moved by music even though it remains a great mystery as to what music is really doing to us.

Most of the symptoms described by psychology are experiences that take place because a person feels out of control. The chaos of anxiety, the immobility of depression, and the slipperiness of madness may be seen as panic responses to the realization that one's life is out of control. Panic may be a wake-up call not just to a neurotic symptom or repressed memory. Spirituality redefines psychological symptoms as opportunities for growth. Psychotherapy, on the other hand, rushes in to help you regain control of your life in the same way that the consumption of alcohol may be used to feed the illusion of control. It ignores the spiritual teaching that is trying to take place—namely the lesson that you never will have much control (or understanding) of your life.

Every moment we succumb to a psychology of repair we ignore our underlying thirst for spirit. Whether inside a therapist's office or inside our own head, we lose an opportunity for spiritual learning. This is not only the case when we are in need of help but also when we position ourselves to rescue others. When others request help and we respond by bringing them back under control through the use of psychological understanding, we avoid trusting the process that is naturally taking place. Without some level of trust, we will always feel anxious and out of control.

♣ When we feel distress and discomfort and turn to psychological understanding to answer why we are in this condition, we set forth on a hunt for someone or something to blame. Once we have named our condition, we have no doubt that there is some agent of harm that caused it. This villain or virus may be in our bloodstream, our genetic material, in our learning, our early childhood experiences, our past or present relationships, in archetypal dramas for which we have been recruited to play a key part. A quick review of the last fifty years demonstrates that the profession of psychology changes its opinion as to what should be blamed about as quickly as fads come through the world of fashion. We have heard about the Oedipus complex, latent homosexuality, inept mothers, abusive fathers, biological origins of depression, borderline and multiple personalities, inner children, and repressed memories to mention a few of the top ten that have arisen as sources of trouble.

Few have stopped to examine the cost of this rigid focus on the hunt for blame. Telling someone in distress that they are ill and that the illness is caused by a psychological or sociological germ sets them up to be dependent upon an expert who becomes a hired gun to track down and exterminate the source of trouble. It sets them up to begin to accommodate this illness by reorganizing relationships around not reawakening the wound. In other words, the illness, or wound, can then take more control over someone's life than it had when the individual was unaware of being ill. Spirituality runs counter to the combative view of pathology. It teaches that the resources to heal are available to us all in our everyday living.

Stepping Outside Understanding and into Intuition

♣ Imagine spending years studying films of swimming, learning the physics of moving bodies in water, becoming aware of all the muscles and biochemical states associated with swimming styles, and gaining familiarity with the biographies of famous Olympic swimmers. The more you learned about swimming, the more you would think there is to understand before you were ready to jump into the water. You could spend a whole lifetime trying to completely understand swimming but never once get wet. The alternative is to simply jump in the water and learn to swim. Forget the understanding, and act. As anyone who has jumped into the pool knows, swimming somehow falls in place.

Learning to swim, ride a bicycle, speak a language, or play a musical instrument takes place naturally. Acquiring knowledge about these learning processes takes us no closer to experience. How we learn to swim as well as learn to live will always be a mystery, never fully realized by our conscious mind.

The bridge to learning has less to do with understanding and more to do with trust. The trust I refer to is a faith based on experience, not a blind faith that follows without question. My wife is a counselor who won't hang up her graduate degrees on her office wall. Instead she displays her birth certificate. It emphasizes her faith in her experience and wisdom rather than her accumulated knowledge. We jump into the water with the trust that our body will find a way to swim. We jump into school with the trust that our mind will find a way to navigate through the maze of texts and examination questions. In some basic sense, we are always ignorant and blind. Yet the gift of trust enables us to hand over our ignorance to the greater whole that lies beyond our limited mind. With this trust we are free to abandon our self and simply jump into the ocean of life. There we move with the current as naturally as all the other waves.

There's an old joke about psychoanalysis, which says that clients, after years of sessions, may not necessarily improve, but they will have a deep understanding of why they haven't changed. I met a client who after years of work with another therapist was no longer concerned that he couldn't keep a relationship or a job. He now understood that it was due to stress caused by growing up in a "dysfunctional family," defined as a household "filled with arguments, tension, and change." His psychological understanding gave him a reason to stay stuck in a situation rather than move toward creating alternative ways of living.

Less Know-It-All and More Trust-in-It-All

✣ The more we believe we can know it all, the less likely we will know anything. When life slams a huge catastrophe in our face, whether it be a serious sickness, loss of a loved one, personal financial disaster, or the destruction of our home by a flood or earthquake, we find that whatever arrogance we hold about security and knowledge is quickly leveled. Catastrophes can be powerful spiritual teachers. We don't have to wait for major catastrophes to level us to spiritual trust and faith: We can choose to bring forth more trust in everything that we do. Notice how trust is already part of your existence. You trust that your body will breathe, even though you may know very little about breathing. Similarly, you trust that you will digest your food and absorb the nutrients you require. You also trust that your body will continue to function while you sleep.

We are as well designed to breathe and digest food as we are to feel the energy of spirit. In the exercises that follow, you will find methods to prepare the ground for coming into closer contact with the soul. Letting go of the need to always understand is one of the most powerful steps toward living a soulful life. Moving from know-it-all understanding to spiritual trust is the bridge that carries you into soulful spirituality.

My friend Ron Geyshick is an Ojibway healer who lives on the Lac La Croix Indian reserve in the Quetico wilderness area of Canada. In a dream he was given some words to help a friend who suffered from a powerful addiction. These words did not tell him that his friend should go to a rehabilitation center. Ron was told to invite his friend to sit still for four days and four nights. When he saw the new moon in the west, this friend was to go into the woods and feed himself. He was to subsequently rest again for four nights and four days, trusting that a spirit would come to guide him. He was to ask it how to help him with his life. If he was lost in the woods, he could ask it for the directions to get home. In this old way of seeking help, he found the spiritual experience that began to heal his addiction.

The spiritual way home has less to do with getting knowledge or finding a solution to a problem. It is more directed at removing yourself from the chatter of everyday life and being still in the midst of mystery.

EXERCISE ONE

Acknowledging the Thirst: Inviting Spirituality into Your Life

✤ You can bring spirituality into your life by simply asking for it to enter. An open heart that moves toward spirit will receive it. Each of us feels the thirst for spirit in the course of every week of our entire life. When we feel that something is missing, that there is more than meets the eye, that there is an unfulfilled longing, an unspecified calling, we are experiencing the thirst for spirit. All of our acts are desperate efforts to satisfy this thirst.

I encourage you to write a letter to your Creator, addressing it by whatever name you feel most comfortable using, whether it's God, Holy Spirit, Allah, the Divine Mother, whatever name you choose. Write God a letter and ask for your life to be blessed, led, and suffused by spirit. Write this letter of request as if your whole life depended on it. Take as much time as you need to do it to the best of your abilities. When your letter is complete, go to a river or natural park area that is nearest to where you live and place your letter in a bottle that you then fill with some water. With this message inside a bottle of water, sprinkle it over yourself and consider this a baptism into a spiritual life.

No matter who you are, a spiritual life is available. When my grandfather was a country preacher, he gave a revival in a town that was harassed by Mr. Black, the local bootlegger. During the evening services, his gang of outlaws would stand outside the church and heckle the congregation. One night my grandfather walked right out of the church and held his Bible over his head, preaching to those men while looking them straight in the eye. They were silenced by his lack of fear, and to everyone's amazement, the notorious Mr. Black returned the following night and was baptized.

The world seems dark outside the peaceful place of our inner temple, but we are called to go outside and stand in faith. This plunge into the darkness of ignorance and discomfort is how we actively invite spirituality into our lives. It is not only the most direct way to awaken our spirit but is the surest way to quench our deepest thirst. Acknowledge your thirst and then step into the places of uncertainty where conventional sense dictates you are unprepared to go. Enter with trust and find the sacred water that is waiting.

EXERCISE TWO

Undermining the Desire to Understand

"If you try to know it, you have already departed from it"
—CHUANG TZU.

☙ It is a "don't know" mind or a beginner's mind that prepares us for the reception of spirit. When we try to understand too much we easily become filled with the mental clutter that impedes our spiritual progress. One of the first steps toward getting free of the potentially debilitating grip of understanding is to begin recognizing how attached to understanding you presently are. For instance, how often do you ask "why" questions rather than "how" questions? Are you more likely to ask, "Why should I?" Or would you be more likely to ask, "How can I?" Catch yourself asking why questions and immediately convert them into being a how question. Use this as a way of initiating more focus on fuller participation in everyday life. Greater participation leads to awakening spirit, not withdrawal from life. The habit of changing the "why's" of your life into "how's" helps plant seeds for action and serves to diminish any distracting weeds of understanding. Here are some examples to help get you thinking in this way:

- Why should I be the one to do it? (How can I do it?)
- Why doesn't he listen to me? (How can I help him listen to me?)
- Why am I stuck in this job? (How can I get moving?)
- Why won't you cooperate? (How can I help you cooperate?)
- Why is there so much evil in the world? (How can I bring more good into my situation?)
- Why are there so many problems? (How can I become a solution?)

Continue examining your life in this way, asking as many questions as you can that will bring forth an awareness of the extent to which you are caught in needing explanations and understanding. In particular, be on the alert for the ways in which your expression and participation in life are impeded by your belief that you don't know enough. When you catch yourself being stopped by these feelings of inadequacy, add this thought to your inner conversation: "I'm aware of my ignorance, which is a sign that there is some don't know mind within my being. This not knowing, according to the great sages of history, is the most perfect preparation for what I feel drawn to become."

Get into the habit of praising the moments when you feel out of control, confused, lost, misunderstood, inadequate, silent, stuck, or bewildered. See these experiences as indicators of an inner not knowing that is the most natural condition you can cultivate for a soulful life. Know that a don't know mind is the stage for spiritual blessings and that deep trust turns on the light so that you may witness them. When you enter life with the stillness of a beginner's don't know mind, and do so with the trust that what is needed will come forth, a great miracle takes place. You lose your ego-centered self in order to facilitate the purest expression of soul.

In the beginning, it may feel strange to think that you should celebrate those times when you feel confused and inadequate. It may even make you more confused to say, "It is good to be confused." But confusion is the beginning of great wisdom. It is not the confusion that you are celebrating, but the fact that the confusion indicates the presence of some don't know mind within you, the ground on which your spirituality can grow.

When we believe that our internal being needs to be filled with knowledge or the possession of some kind of experience, we may enter the paradoxical dance of addiction. We seek to fill our internal emptiness, only to find that each filling makes us less satisfied. So off we go to fill it again, whether it be with alcohol, possessions, or the elixirs of understanding. The thirst that we are unable to quench is a thirst for realizing our natural state of well-formed emptiness and not knowing. In this space, spirit may fill us with the light that awakens the depths of our soul. Here we may find utter bliss that takes us beyond all craving and suffering. It's not always easy to get to, but the spiritual light is there to help us.

THE UNQUENCHABLE THIRST 19

As you begin to cultivate a new respect for your ignorance, inadequacy, and discomfort, you will be less worried about whether you feel understood by others or whether you understand them. You will worry less about whether you have the talent, training, or aptitude to do something, whether it be playing a musical instrument, writing a poem, being a parent, or learning a new skill. You will be less interested in hearing explanations that account for who you are and will feel less inclined to believe that others would change if you could deliver to them the right understanding of things. In these ways your understanding will become undermined, freeing you to participate in the how of living rather than the why of understanding.

EXERCISE THREE

The Return to Stillness:
Being Present Rather than Reactive

❦ It's the little habits that often get us down. Like the way we react to other people when they push our buttons. We feel and display irritation over things that don't really matter. We lose our tempers when our spouse forgets to put the cap back on the toothpaste, shout at our children when they leave a lunch box at a friend's house, or stress out over a favorite team's loss. These little habits of impatient reactions take their toll on our life and busy our inner mind with too much noise and small talk. There's a bigger toll: They lay the ground for more of this behavior in the future. Every action becomes a seed that will sprout.

Begin appreciating the difference between reacting to life as opposed to being present with it. When you automatically react, your emotions jump in without being aware of what's really happening. It's as if the world's outside stimuli are directly wired to your inner responses. This kind of response makes you a victim of what is going on outside of you.

Couples and families can often trace the tensions and difficulties of everyday life to these little habits of reaction. One partner doesn't even have to finish a statement before the other one has reacted. It may have been the tone of the other person's voice that sets off the reactionary alarm or perhaps the way their eye made a certain glance or the tilt of their head flashed a signal. When couples overlook these little habits, they may easily get lost in a lot of meaningless content, where the unattainable phrase of understanding that is supposed to patch their life together becomes the focus rather than adjusting the reactionary processes that have a tight grip on them.

The alternative to a reactionary response is to be fully present to the situation in a way that stems from an inner stillness and an outer awareness that is clear and nonjudgmental. Living in the spiritual stream moves you out of reactions and into pure presence. Without the stillness that that presence brings about, there is no way to hear the inner guidance offered by spirit. If you are doing nothing but reacting to the stimuli around you, then you are not fully present with body, mind, and soul. You are only renting out your body so that it can exercise some prewired programming.

Give yourself a special time during each day that you devote to being more aware of your habitual reactions. Begin to notice what the cues or signals are that trigger them to take place. Purchase a pocket-size clicker toy so that as you become aware of the external signals that start to trigger an automatic reaction, you can reach for your clicker and make three clicks. As you hear this sound, regard it as a wake-up call to be more present and less reactive to the moment.

Inserting a sound, a saying, tying your shoes, fixing your eyes on an object, moving your little finger into your habitual responses wake you up from the trance of reactive behavior and free you to be more alive in the present. When you do so, you will feel better without the residues of frustration, irritability, and anger that typically accompany reactionary habits.

In addition to introducing more of these wake-up calls into your life, become more mindful of the state of mind that full presence brings about. The truest meditation is to be in this state of presence during the course of your everyday challenges. It's one thing to remain quiet and still on the inside when it's quiet and still on the outside, but try doing it when there is external noise that challenges you to react. This is the deep work where the meditation hall is found in your everyday life.

The idea of being fully present is expressed by the Taoist notion of *wu-wei,* which refers to "not forcing yourself." When you go against the grain, swim against the current, or react against the provocation, you are forcing yourself as opposed to simply being with the present flow of life. This latter way of being is as flexible as a willow branch that yields to the weight of snow or the force of the wind not because it is passive but because it is springy and able to move as the situation calls for it to do so. The fourth-century Chinese philosopher Lieh-Tzu, when captured by this presence in the flow, said, "I knew not whether the wind was riding on me or I on the wind."

As you behold rather than interpret, evaluate, and judge, mystery makes itself present. True presence is nothing less than entry into the mystery of life. Here we stand with a sense of wonder and enchantment, beholding what no mortal could ever hope to control, understand, or handle. We are brought before the altar of life where the limitations of our mind are sacrificed so that the seeing of a greater mind is present.

EXERCISE FOUR

Letting in Love

☙ An awakened heart is a necessary condition for being able to receive the light.

Consider choosing three days where you pay special attention to any appropriate living creature, whether it be your spouse, parent, child, friend, pet, or plant. Imagine that these are the last three days you will be with them. Tell them that you are taking three days to conduct a spiritual experiment and that they are not to have any unnecessary concern about your actions. Repeat this every other month until it is a bimonthly holy day for you. Watch how the practice of love's actions helps deepen your preparation to encounter the light and enrich your every day.

The value of practicing the love that opens your heart is illustrated by the story of a solitary dog who spent the last three days of his life being awakened by the generosity of a lonely man.

One day while walking through a park, an old crippled dog came up to an old man who had never experienced love in his entire life. The dog caught his attention by speaking these words, "I am old and crippled. Children don't like to look at me because I look so sick and pitiful. I only have three days left to live, and more than anything else in the world, I long to have the experience of being loved by my master. I want this so much that I have learned how to speak so someone could hear my request. I have searched the world for a person who would understand my situation, and I think you understand what it is like not to have love in your life. Would you please grant me my wish that you be a good master to me in my last three days? You don't have to really love me. It would be fine for you to pretend that you love me."

The old man was moved by the sincerity of the dog's request. Without deliberation he told that dog that he would give him the best three days of his life. Off they went on a great three-day adventure. The old man took him to a restaurant and fed him a delicious steak, showed him all the beautiful places in the park, and took him to the spots that had unique odors and smells. The old creature was permitted to sleep on his master's bed, and throughout the night the man rubbed his belly and sang him soothing songs.

At the end of the three days, the dog said to the old man, "You have truly cared for me and I am most grateful. You have enabled me to open my heart. For the first time I know what it feels like to love someone." The old man began weeping and replied, "I, too, have learned to love and have never felt more alive." At that moment a shaft of bright white light entered the old man's apartment window and transformed itself into a staircase to the sky. A voice from above was heard by all the neighbors, "Come, both of you, unto my house. You have prepared the ground for your hearts to enter the kingdom of light." The old man with the dog by his side walked all the way up that staircase of light and disappeared into the clouds.

It is said that all love dogs know this story and to this day they look to the sky when they howl their song. They haven't forgotten that it requires a heart filled with longing and love to enter the light of the heavens.

Sultan Walad, the son of Rumi, speaks to us about this new life in soul:

"A human being must be born twice. Once from his mother, and again from his own body and his own existence. The body is like an egg, and the essence of man must become a bird in that egg through

the warmth of love, and then he can escape from his body and fly in
the eternal world of the soul beyond time and space."

   You enter the soulful flight to bring spirited life into your daily
action. You earn your wings through the heartfelt practice of love. This
is how your life is illumined by spirit and how you become a midwife
to the birth of everyday soul.

CHAPTER TWO

❧

Making Grace out of Life's Disturbances

The value of human life lies in the fact of suffering, for where there is no suffering . . . there can be no power of attaining spiritual experience . . . Unless we agree to suffer we cannot be free from suffering.

—D. T. SUZUKI

WHILE I WAS a graduate student in clinical psychology my life was interrupted by the disturbing arrival of anxiety attacks. When the attack would sneak up on me, I would have to stop whatever I was doing. If I were driving a car, I would have to pull over to the side of the road and wait until it passed. There were times I would have to run out of the classroom because of the loss of equilibrium the anxiety brought. Sometimes these panic episodes were so intense I feared I was having a heart attack.

No matter what book I read about anxiety, it didn't help. Whether I read Carl Jung or Karen Horney, it kept me more aware of the existence of anxiety in my life, and this tended to make it more present. Even thinking or talking about it could make me anxious. My experience with therapists was essentially the same as reading self-help and professional books. Although they might provide a moment of relief during the sessions when the therapists took over worrying about it, they more often than not brought me deeper into the mesmerizing spell that the disturbance held over my life.

I was fortunate to come across the work of the radical psychiatrist R. D. Laing, who embraced the disturbances of life as an opportunity for personal development and growth. In the spirit of his approach I decided to become a student of my symptom, to learn from it, and be guided by the way it was opening a new world of consciousness I had never experienced before.

I readied myself to make a study of this whirling inner experience, observe its vibrations, the quality of its tingliness and dizziness, assess its duration, tempo, and rhythms, become aware of how it alters my visual, auditory, and tactile experiences, pay attention to whether it was localized on any particular parts of my body, and note how it affected my heart, body temperature, and gastrointestinal system. I waited to explore the next entry into anxious consciousness. In this preparation I shifted my relationship with anxiety to becoming more curious about it rather than fearing it as I had before. I never had another anxiety attack. In this encounter with anxiety, I learned one of the greatest secrets of life. Changing your relationship to a symptom is the key to transforming it into a graceful outcome. Understanding the cause of your symptom, distress, problem, confusion, difficulty, discomfort, or dis-ease does not necessarily change anything. In fact, a deeper plunge into understanding your symptom often gives it too much attention and contributes to its becoming bigger than life. You become drawn into making it more real and powerful than it actually need be and concretizing it as a deeply engrained part of your life.

One of the biggest traps we fall into is that we look for the origins of what we find disturbing as if it were a medical disease rather than an emotional state of dis-ease. Even the choice to give a disturbing experience a pathological name, like "symptom" or "problem," takes us further into a dark and immobilizing view of our condition and situation. When we pathologize our life, we become like an architect who designs a psychological structure for imprisoning our potential to move forward. As a victim of a symptom, it naturally follows that we will be dominated by a fear of the condition returning. What we fail to see is how the power of a symptom derives from the way we feed our fear of it. We fail to trust life and the processes it uses to teach and guide us.

The way out involves no particular understanding of your past or present situation, but a change in how you relate to it. In my own personal encounter with anxiety, I moved from a terrified fear to a mobilized curiosity, and that was enough to take away the potency of its powerful grip. There are endless ways of relating to the disturbances that enter our life. However, any response that sets us up to conquer and eradicate the problem may paradoxically make it more present and discomforting. Any way of relating to the symptom that brings forth more imaginative and resourceful responses will not only loosen its grip but may very well result in gracing the quality of our life.

The mistake we make with discomforting experience is that we try to beat it rather than join it. We go to war with our discomfort, first giving it a name that justifies our going into psychological or medical warfare with it. The main reason people are in trouble and end up going to a therapist is that they have already been doing psychology with their life and have spent weeks, months, and even longer trying to fight their symptom. The last thing needed is an escalation of this warfare with one's inner life.

Everyday soul is about fully attending to what is present and finding a way to resourcefully relate to it so as to bring forth a graceful outcome, even when this involves the most difficult and painful circumstances. Everything in life is a teacher with a lesson that is perfectly made for you during the time in which it is received. We are never given more than we can bear. Grace, the divine presence and generosity of spirit, befalls those whose hands are open to receive it. The work of spirit is toward making graceful outcomes and blessing all that we receive in life. It steps away from seeing problems that need to be solved and difficulties that must be surmounted. Spirituality embraces all of life, its upsides and downsides, and does so with the serenity and calmness of a still but powerful compassion for the whole of creation.

The Alchemy of Change

♣ A soulful approach to life does not fight the disturbances that come to you. It invites you to find a way to transform them into grace. The legendary psychotherapist Milton H. Erickson mastered this way of utilizing symptoms. He once treated a twenty-two-year-old man who had been biting his nails since he was four. He originally bit them until they bled, hoping it would get him out of practicing the piano, but his mother made him practice anyway. He then grew up to flunk out of two medical schools and finally saw Milton Erickson at the insistence of his father. Rather than ask, "Why do you think you're biting your nails" or "How do you feel when you bite them," Erickson suggested he let one nail grow long so he could enjoy the pleasure of chewing on a long, juicy one. The man grew the nail but refused to bite it. He then grew all his nails, stopped biting them, began playing the organ as a hobby, and completed law school.

There was an institutionalized patient in a midwestern psychiatric institution diagnosed as psychotic. He was given this label because the mental-health professionals didn't know how else to understand a man who stood all day making a back-and-forth movement with his arms and hands, uttering only: "I am Jesus Christ."

A visiting consultant said to him, "I hear you're Jesus and that you're a carpenter. It looks like you're missing a saw. Let me see what we can do about that." He then arranged to place a saw in the man's hands and to have someone hold lumber so that the man's arm movements now became the action of sawing wood. As a carpenter who was once missing a saw, he was now engaged in resourceful conduct. This patient began making a bookcase and eventually was discharged from the hospital, pursuing a career as a cabinetmaker.

In a similar fashion, the psychotherapist R. D. Laing was introduced to a young woman who had been diagnosed as a catatonic schizophrenic, meaning she would go into frozen postures for long periods of time. When he met her, he said, "I hear you have a talent for being still." He then persuaded her to use this ability to get a job as a model posing in an art studio. The same behavior that others used to impoverish the meaning of her life was transformed into a profitable resource, helping move her life toward a successful future.

"Use what you have to work with" not only applies to coaching a sports team but directs how we can most gracefully play the game of life.

Constructing Your Reality

♣ The biologist John Lilly recorded the word "cogitate" on a tape over and over again: cogitate, cogitate, cogitate, cogitate . . . After several moments of listening to this tape, people began hearing other words. At a conference of the American Society of Linguistics, Lilly played the tape, and the group heard some 2,361 different words and word combinations: agitate; arbitrate; artistry; back and forth; candidate; can't you stay; catch a tape; conscious state; count to ten; Cape Cod, you say; cut a steak; got a date; got to take; gurgitate; marmalade . . .

What we perceive is a consequence of how we participate in perceiving. With respect to Lilly's experiment, a person's report of what is heard reveals more about how the observer is observing than what is actually on the tape. For instance, when played to neurophysiologists, the most frequently heard word was "computate," whereas for therapists working in mental hospitals the most frequently heard word was "tragedy." Lilly remarked that when he presents the tape to an audience with which he hasn't achieved a good rapport, he himself hears "stop the tape."

Life itself is like an endless tape that repeats the same sound. What we hear, see, and feel are therefore statements about our participation in life rather than any objective representation of what is really happening to us. We are not passive recipients of life but active constructors of our experience. When we see problems, trauma, and shortcomings, we are acting in such a way as to bring forth that realization through a self-fulfilling prophecy. Spirituality invites us to act in such a way as to bring forth the spiritual gifts of healing, reconciliation, forgiveness, blessings, and peace.

When a person tells me that they have "depression," I usually ask them who told them so or what it is that makes them believe this is the case. They eventually respond with simple descriptions of their difficulties such as, "I have trouble getting up in the morning," "I don't know whether I can keep a job," "I worry too much about my kids," or "I feel heavy and slow." When I shift to these specifics of their day-to-day lives, I find that it is easier to come up with some fresh ideas that might be useful, whereas a focus on an abstract concept like "depression" is less resourceful. It tends to explain why their life is miserable without giving a clue what might be done differently.

We are too often stuck in seeing the world in only one way and forget that we can be led to different viewings. A wealthy oil baron once commissioned Picasso to paint a portrait of his wife. When the work was completed, the baron was shocked to see the image that had been created. "Why that looks nothing like my wife! You should have painted her the way she really is!" Picasso took a deep breath and said, "I'm not sure what that would be." Without hesitation, the oil baron pulled out his wallet and removed a photograph of his wife saying, "There, you see, this is a picture of how she really is!" Picasso, bending over, looked at it and replied, "She is rather small and flat, isn't she?"

The great spiritual traditions have always taught that much of what we hold as true objective reality is but an illusion created by the hand that serves the eye beholding it. Drawing the world in terms of pathology sets us up to be held down in the darkness, unable to see the spiritual resources that surround us. I am not suggesting that people suffer only because they see themselves as suffering. What I'm saying is that there are many ways to relate to our suffering.

We do not need to be less compassionate toward suffering but become more compassionate and hopeful about the ways in which suffering can be a spiritual teacher. This is the awareness that psychology too often forgets. Seeing the psychopathologies of everyday life as conditions of spiritual dis-ease moves us to a higher ground where we may relate to them in a more transformative way.

Each of us goes through the day proving to ourselves that life is exactly as we believe it to be. We punctuate the endless "cogitates" in such a way that we hear what we believe must be present. In this way, our beliefs are always kept true, even when they are not. For instance, if you rigorously demand that your spouse be more loving to you, then you may not believe that the forthcoming overtures of kindness are authentic. You may snap back with words like, "You're only giving me flowers because I asked you to, not because you really want to!" or "If you really loved me, I wouldn't have to question it." If you truly believe you are not loved, nothing anyone else does can prove otherwise.

Everyday life is sprinkled with vicious circles that keep us locked into nonresourceful conduct. For deeply engrained pessimists, no data can shift them away from their darkened outlook. If it's sunny, they'll say, "But it won't last," or "It reminds me of how much I miss the sun whenever it rains." It is possible to release virtuous circles into our performance of everyday life. We can choose to enjoy the sun when it comes out. To such a person, both rain and sunshine are embraced and celebrated, evil and good are accepted as teachers, and sickness and health are understood as guides to life.

Accepting and Transforming What Comes to You

❧ One of my teachers, the Zulu spiritual leader Vusamazulu Credo Mutwa, was once told by a doctor that he would soon die because of a cancer named melanoma. Credo began laughing and responded, "Why that sounds like the name of a beautiful woman. Am I going to be killed by this goddess?" He told the doctor that he was not going to be killed by Melanoma because he would dedicate himself to honoring her. He immersed himself in sculpting a gigantic statue of a goddess. He worked day and night and was completely overtaken by it. He was so weak at times that his friends had to lift him in order for him to complete the work. To the surprise of the doctors, the malignant lesions disappeared.

The purest and truest spiritual life begins with accepting everything that comes to you as a gift and teaching. As Mother Teresa reminds us, this includes sickness and all possible misfortunes. The most difficult times sometimes bring the most important teachings. Each lesson is another step toward learning how to accept what comes to us as material to be transformed into the grace of spiritual light.

There is an old saying that "for any great truth, its opposite is also true." Furthermore, indulging in one side of a distinction or duality eventually leads to bringing forth what has been hidden in its other side. For example, the more you try to make yourself go to sleep, the more awake you may become. Or the more a do-gooder fights evil, the more likely they will eventually spend the night embracing it, as we've seen with some of the more flamboyant television evangelists.

The analogy of changing the course of a river is often used to explain how this transformational tactic works. If you try to directly change the river's path by opposing it, the water will go right over you. But if you accept the river's flow and divert it in a different direction, it will carve out a new channel. When applied to negative habits, the inertia of an ongoing habit will override any effort you make to directly oppose it. But if you move with the habit and offer a slight variation, it will begin to shift itself into a new pattern of behavior. Like the martial art of judo, you accept the motion of your opponent and utilize it.

My mother is an elementary school principal who was once presented with a child who would not stop disrupting the classroom by imitating animal sounds. The teacher tried numerous discipline tactics and asked for the help of the school psychologist. When their efforts were defeated, he was sent to the principal's office. My mother surprised him by not scolding his conduct but by expressing curiosity about his rumored talent. She urged him to perform his animal impressions for her so she could hear how skilled he was at doing it. When he finally made a few grunts, she encouraged him to be in the school talent show so that he could display his act for all the children to enjoy. The boy never made another noise in that classroom but began exploring ways in which he could excel as a performer in socially appropriate settings such as school plays, choir, and dramatic readings.

I once worked with a young college student who couldn't stop thinking that her life was hopeless and that nothing positive would ever come about. I encouraged her to escalate this despair until she was able to say, "It's become so hopeless, there's nothing I can do. Therefore why not have one last fantasy before I completely give up?" I then recommended that she fantasize about a life she would want to have should she die and become reincarnated as a highly evolved spiritual person.

Her fantasy, which involved being a children's poet, was regarded as an imaginary "flashforward" (as opposed to "flashback") experience. I subsequently arranged for a photograph to be taken of her while she showed her best "flashforward expression." She looked full of happiness. She found that she could benefit from taking a peek at this photograph, and her hopelessness began to lift.

I also saw a middle-aged man who had been diagnosed and medicated for "clinical depression." In our first meeting he described how he was totally committed to living a spiritual life and that he presently was working for a Christian mission. He went on to recite some biblical scripture and to say that although the psychiatrists had done their best, his depression was getting worse.

I asked him whether he had considered a spiritual aspect to his depression, reminding him that everything that happened in his life was obviously related to his spirituality. He was quite surprised to hear this question, given that all his previous encounters with mental health professionals had focused on the biological reality of his depression. He gathered himself and said that he and his wife had once tried to understand why God had brought this upon them. When I asked what it felt like to have depression, he said it made him feel very heavy; sometimes he had difficulty getting out of bed in the morning.

We discussed how Jesus must have felt as he carried the burdens of the world. The man said that all disciples and followers of Jesus must accept the way of their Savior and carry the cross. I asked the man whether it was possible that his depression might also be a spiritual teaching, through which he could learn more about what it feels like to carry a heavy cross. God may have decided to give him this experience as a way of coming closer to his spirituality. As this theme was developed, the man began to see his depression as a spiritual resource and teaching.

We were able to design a task that involved his building a wooden cross that he would keep in his house. Whenever he felt the heaviness come over him, he was to lie down in bed and place the cross on top of himself. As he did this, he was to imagine how it must have been for Jesus to have carried the weight of the cross.

His feelings of depression now brought the man to a closer relationship with Jesus, and enabled him to feel spiritually empowered. The man was able to lift himself out of his depression by using it to tap into the strength and power of his spirituality.

Everyday life presents us with a choice: Do we see problems and difficulties that need to be conquered and solved or do we see opportunities for making grace? The highest spiritual call is not about alleviating suffering but embracing and transforming it into the grace of spiritual light. This is why we are here—to serve in the creation of light and to live and bathe in its illumination.

EXERCISE ONE

A Past Fast

✣ George Bernard Shaw once quipped that "the only lesson we learn from history is that we learn nothing from history." Reflecting upon our personal history as a means of understanding ourselves often leads us to making excuses for why we are destined to stay stuck in repeating our past. We too often believe that who we are is caused by who we were and then we fall into proving the truth of our past by recycling it into our present. As the karmic recycling of biographies, we dwell more upon the problems of the past and are less free to imagine making spiritual grace.

Perhaps the only way we can appreciate a past-free life is to consider what it would be like to have no past. This condition frees you from the past without having any responsibility for remembering. If you have truly forgotten your past, you are fully in the present, unencumbered by the hold of memories that call out for self-verfying actions.

Set aside a time to imagine what your life would be like if you were to wake up with amnesia. You would face each relationship, job task, play, and dream without any assumptions of how these things fit into your life before. Every day would be a new beginning, and in the purest sense, you would experience yourself being continuously reborn.

I have a friend who is a nurse and in her free time she loves to dance. When she does this exercise she wakes up with the belief that she never has seen a patient before and that she never has taken a single dance step. She readies herself in the morning by pretending that she is thrilled to be on her way to see her first patient. As she waits for her morning coffee, she turns on some music and takes a few steps as if it were her first experience with dance. She goes through the entire day seeing, hearing, tasting, smelling, and touching the world in this way that is free from past expectations and evaluative comparisons. It becomes a way of bringing back her don't know mind. It keeps her work fresh, compassionate, and open to endless possibility.

While you reflect on the absence of your past, imagine you could actually remove, with surgical precision, three events from the past. No longer would these events be part of your memory nor would any residual effects play themselves out in any way. Write down a brief sentence for each historical event. Read each out loud with the commitment that this will be the last time you ever give any credence to the power of this past event. As you read this sentence, think about how the past is held in language. Without being able to say it, internally or externally, it could not be grasped. It evaporates, just like a dream upon waking.

Now write down each sentence in reverse. Start with the last letter of the last word and reverse the entire sentence. Say this out loud every day for a week and then cross out the last word. Do this every week until all the backward words have been eliminated. Imagine that saying the reverse form is a way of undoing and erasing that aspect of your past that has been held in your memory through words. Without the words, these events do not exist.

Practice this ritual whenever you want to become freer from your psychological history. Use it when you get bogged down in an old anger or resentment, or you find yourself getting involved with the wrong person yet again. Clearing out these internal obstacles is essential to preparing the way for spirit.

Begin a lifestyle where you give at least one hour if not one day per week to being free from the past. Call it your past fast. During that time you can not say anything about the past, reflect upon it, or be organized by whatever understandings come from it. Explore different ways of fasting from your past. These may include doing something you have never done in the past. It may be a small change like looking up an entry in the encyclopedia you've never read before or trying a different food at a restaurant you have never frequented. Buy a recording you've never heard, say something out loud that you never uttered before, smile in a different way, make an unusual sound, hand gesture, walking style in a way that doesn't fit the way you ever did it in the past.

As you set aside a specific time every week to fast from the past, think of it as temporal dieting. In a sense, you are shedding time from your mind, enabling it to be more open and empty. Letting go of the past prepares you for being present now. The Divine Light exists in the eternal present, and you must be in the present to receive it. Anything that shakes you free from past habits and moves you into the freshness of the present will help ready you for spiritual encounter.

You may want to go on an actual dietary restriction for that day, giving up any dessert or high-calorie items for the time you are doing your past fast. This will empower the fast. Feeling physically lighter may help you feel lighter in every other way.

When you find that a memory slips into your consciousness, respond to it as if someone else told you that this had happened in your past. Ask yourself, "How can I really know that took place?" If you had amnesia, you would doubt whether reports of your past were true. If you were remembering a dream, you would know you weren't chased by a monster or didn't actually fall off a cliff, or didn't say those things to your boss that would jeopardize your job. Relate to your past as if it were as slippery as a dream.

If we assume that there can be such a thing as repressed trauma, then it logically holds that we could also have repressed bliss. Repressed bliss is an experience of happiness so intense and fantastic that you have to forget about it because otherwise it might overwhelm your present state of mind. As you play with your past, consider uncovering repressed memories of blissful experience. Bring them back into your awareness as a means of discovering that it is not only advisable to follow your own bliss, it also is pleasing to find the bliss that already resides within you.

Time and history are no different than the ever-repeating tape of "cogitate." What we remember is brought forth by how we punctuate the multileveled, richly textured, polyphonic past. The past is a consequence of how we act in the present. Amnesia, real or pretended, provides us with a metaphorical way of erasing the slate and encourages us to come up with something fresh. Use this new beginning as an opportunity to invite more grace into your life.

Starting Off Small

♣ The most effective way to bring a larger grace into your life is to begin with releasing small, graceful outcomes into your everyday activities. Consider how a small snowball rolling down a mountain becomes a gigantic ball, possibly leading to an avalanche of change. Or to use the analogy of a hole in a dam; a very small hole can lead to the whole dam being restructured. We, too, easily become distracted by trying to bring about large successes all at once, forgetting that the surest way to get there is to let a small, graceful outcome roll along and naturally realize our hopes, aspiration, and dreams.

Begin by making an inventory of the areas where small, graceful outcomes can be made—in the workplace, relationships and home life, recreation, rest, play, community involvement, and so forth. Perhaps these will include placing an interesting item on your office desk, an extra dose of humor in the homefront, an additional five minutes of exercise and relaxation, or making one call a month to someone involved in community politics. These outcomes do not have to be seen by anyone else as important or even as making sense.

As a warmup to releasing little doses of grace into your life, begin by flooding your world with all kinds of tiny changes. Change all the pencils and pens in your home or workplace and then find and start using an inspiring word you seldom use. Make a small rearrangement of something in your bedroom. You might reverse the way you place your pillows or decorate your dresser with one flower or even a single blade of grass. Add some healthy and delicious food to your refrigerator that has never been there before. Come up with a kind social greeting that you have never used with your colleagues at work and try it out on them. Instead of saying, "Hi, how are you?" maybe you want to try, "It's great seeing you today."

Develop a new way of thinking about change and success. Imagine that every small difference you actually introduce into your life brings some spiritual grace into your life. It not only releases a change into the world, it helps open your mind and helps you achieve that state of spiritual emptiness, or don't know mind, that is capable of holding spiritual experience. As more of these changes are set forth, they will become a powerful force that will carry all of your deepest dreams forward with them. You will find the power of making the big dreams come true by strictly focusing on the small and particular moments that hold the whole of your existence.

As you bring small, graceful outcomes into the world, see yourself as a kind of Johnny Appleseed of change, spreading seeds wherever you go. Know that a great seeding is needed before a magnificent forest can be realized. At the end of each day, replace your worrying and concerns with reflecting upon what seeds of grace you can plant when you get up in the morning. See every seed as helping move the whole of your life toward a marvelous blossoming.

Why not purchase a collection of real seeds, comprising a wide variety of beautiful flowers, and end each day by taking out the number of seeds that correspond to the number of seeds of grace you planted that day? Place these seeds in a special jar and watch them accumulate over time. Consider actually planting these seeds in the ground and witnessing the miracle of growth. Imagine how enriched your life would be by seeing the flowers you helped bring into the earth as well as into the lives of others.

EXERCISE THREE

Recycling Yourself

✤ Encourage yourself to practice the recycling of your daily life. This refers to a way of spiritually and emotionally digesting the experiences of each day, becoming nourished by their resources, and letting everything else pass through. All experiences carry both resourceful nutrients as well as waste products. Without the nutrients we suffer from malnutrition, and without letting go of the waste we become poisoned. The art of recycling yourself and creating graceful outcomes involves keeping the positive and resourceful aspects and letting go of the negative and toxic wastes.

Choose a special place in your home where you may sit for contemplation. When you come home from work, sit in the chair and reflect upon all the experiences that came to you during the course of the day. Now say to yourself something like, "It is now time to digest the experiences of the day. I hold them all within me and want to keep what is nutritious and vital for my well-being and release all that should be passed on."

Within your mind's eye, see all of your experiences turning into multicolored vapors. With this image, begin blowing strong puffs of wind into the air in front of you and imagine that you are mixing all of the vapors together as one composite vapor. See this vapor as white but containing dark spots. The white consists of all the happiness, bliss, and good feelings that you felt during the day, while the dark spots comprise all the negative emotions or events. Take a deep breath and bring the white part of the vapor deeply into your body. When you breathe out, imagine that you are releasing and blowing away the dark spots.

Think of the white vapor as all that is essential from the sum total of your daily experiences and the dark spots as that which is toxic and needs to be passed on. Take twelve breaths in this way and then be still as you imagine the white vapor spontaneously and effortlessly moving through every limb, organ, bone, blood vessel, and cell of your body.

When this has been completed, use your hands to gently pat your body. Do this as a means of keeping in the white nutrients and closing off any re-entry of the dark toxins. Perform this practice on a daily basis, allowing at least five minutes for the recycling to take place. You may also do this recycling procedure whenever something powerful happens to you, whether it be the announcement of some sad news, a disagreement, the thrill of winning a game, or the excitement of seeing a great movie. When a strong emotion enters your everyday life, consider going to a private place and doing the recycling meditation.

As you become familiar and comfortable with this practice, it will take place without effort and provide a natural way of bathing your mind, cleansing it each day after returning home from the workplace. It may be best to do this before you talk with your family or friends because it helps purify you from the toxins of work that sometimes contaminate your relationships and evening life at home. You may also repeat this practice as many times as you need during the day. Although you may do it at work, while commuting, or during a brisk walk, you should always remember to do it on a daily basis in your special place at home.

Over time, you may begin seeing each breath you take as an ongoing recycling process. See the light of each breath as coming from the sacred light. Believe that your breath brings you closer to being spiritually awakened by turning your everyday emotions and experiences into light.

EXERCISE FOUR

Hatching Your Bliss

❧ Immediately pause and ask yourself what you believe would bring forth the deepest bliss in your life. Joseph Campbell's advice to follow your own bliss requires that we first fantasize what we think our bliss would be if it were available to us. Is it singing a song with such musical purity that it lifts us into the clouds? Or does your bliss have to do with how you play with your children, cook a special meal, dance throughout the night, write a poem, cultivate a great garden, or engage in a voyage around the world?

Whatever you believe constitutes a definition of your bliss, write it down on a piece of white paper. Cut this paper into an oval shape so that it resembles an egg. Carefully place this egg under your bed, directly underneath where your heart resides when you sleep. Tonight when you go to sleep, see yourself as a mother hen resting over an egg, waiting for it to hatch. Know that clues may be born into your imagination that direct you to take some steps toward finding your bliss.

This hatching may take place in your dreams, where you'll be told or shown something about moving toward your bliss. Or it may pop into your mind unexpectedly during the forthcoming days. Be mindful of trying to hatch your egg and wonder when the miracle of birth will take place. Anticipate the hatching of your bliss as a major spiritual blessing in your life. Prepare for it the same way you would for a new arrival in your home.

Invent your future spiritual grace and place it in the egg in this way, waiting for some guidance to be delivered that will help you move toward realizing it. This practice is a powerful bridge for entering the deepest parts of your imagination, the sacred well that holds all the answers and direction you need. Use it to help bring forth the dreams that will move you into the bliss of soulful living.

Spirituality does not cover its eyes to the suffering, agony, and pain of the world. It embraces it with open arms and transforms it with compassion and love. When suffering is wed with the joyous love of the heart, the sacred light is born, giving rebirth and rejuvenation to all who are touched by it. We must see the suffering as well as the bliss in our lives and bring them together. Follow your bliss and follow your suffering. At their intersection you will find the Divine Light.

CHAPTER THREE

❧

Tripping Your Self:
The Spirited Performance of
Crazy Wisdom

Eternity is a mere moment, just long enough for a joke.

—HERMAN HESSE

To remain whole, be twisted.
To become straight, let yourself be bent.
To become full, be hollow.

—TAO TE CHING

THE SMALL TOWN I grew up in was filled with eccentric characters, people who stepped outside
the boundaries that circumscribe the status quo. I'll never forget Robin
Lewis, the town inventor and poet, who converted a steam locomotive
into a vehicle that could sail down the highway and who in the midst
of a snowstorm would glide over the ice in the kind of airboat you see
in the Florida Everglades. I grew up realizing that the most precious
jewels to behold were people who didn't care about fitting the average
social mold but dared to dance to the calling of their own music. My
family thrived on reviewing what the local characters were up to, and

though we may not have been aware of it at the time, they encouraged us to develop our own unique ways of being in the world.

Smithville, Missouri, was a *Waltons* kind of place where I was awakened each morning by the clanging sounds coming from the neighboring blacksmith shop, a place where some of the wildest contraptions you ever saw and the wildest stories you ever heard were built from scratch. The parsonage we lived in was also next door to a house the neighborhood children believed was haunted, but it actually held two elderly sisters, one of whom never spoke a word and never came outside. The only sign that she had life took place when she occasionally burst into music on the piano, which could happen any time of the day or night.

We didn't always have to look to our neighbors for character. My mother's father was an out-of-the-ordinary inventor, farmer, and construction worker who would farm acres of land with crops that weren't supposed to grow in the region. I remember when the local state university sent down some agricultural scientists to see how he could grow a healthy crop of sugar cane outside of the tropics. Even when he was too feeble to walk, he would plant and harvest his crop by crawling on the ground. Nothing stopped him from his annual rituals, including his yearly ordeal of taking his outdated Corvair apart, piece by piece, and then putting it back together again. He did this before driving each summer to visit his sister in Georgia, where he grew up.

When Auburn, as he was called, decided to move out of the family mobile home and build a house, he did so without a blueprint. Although it had one odd corner that eventually held the television set, it came out exactly as he wanted.

My uncle Zane Rex Gnann lived with my grandparents. He was an idiot savant. He could remember the serial number of any key ever made, and compute a monthly bank interest statement to the third decimal point. Zane was also an epileptic. Grandpa's mynah bird would cry out his name just minutes before he would have a seizure. When you heard that bird shout, "Zaaaannnnee," the children would take cover while the adults helped Zane get ready for his episode.

PaPa, my father's father, was once the pastor to Auburn, my grandmother Bess, and Zane in a small town located in the "boot heel" of Missouri. PaPa always wore a suit, even when he mowed the yard. He served the poor and the hard-working members of that community but did so dressed like a duke. His wife, Virginia, sang in the church choir, taught Sunday school, gave piano lessons, and kept everyone laughing. My sister and I called her "Doe" because being with her was as freeing as running through the woods with a wild and beautiful deer.

Everywhere you looked in my childhood, there were colorful lives. I grew up believing that life required a healthy dose of eccentricity. My family, friends, and neighbors taught me that we are free to choose any role, performance, or style of living and that life is, without question, enhanced by the kind of wisdom that derives from being outside the mainstream, having what has been called "crazy wisdom." It is the wisdom of the eccentric, the outsider, the poet, the Zen master, the saint, and the sacred fool.

The crazy-wisdom view notices that the emperor wears no clothes and that that is fine. It is aware that much of our everyday habits are based on irrational assumptions. Relishing paradox, surprise, and laughter, it provides the necessary balance to overseriousness, stuffy piety, and rigid thinking. Often rebellious, it challenges the conventional wisdom of the habitual, unexamined life.

I tried out many roles and performances in my own life. When I was a child, my parents allowed me to move into the basement, where I built a labyrinth of rooms, including a library, music studio, and two laboratories. I convinced junkyards and government surplus stores to donate all sorts of equipment to me, and I managed to acquire a radar station and the power transformer of an electron microscope, not to mention the basic tools for conducting chemical investigations. When a train wreck spilled electronic equipment all over the place, I was there to collect it, and when the leading town physician passed away, I inherited his medical library.

It was quite a shock to begin college and not find myself hidden in a lab. College was less about inventing and creating, and more about memorizing the right answers to the tests. I conformed to this ordeal for one year with straight A's in all my courses, but I rebelled against the system by starting an underground student newspaper that upset some of the faculty and students so much that they asked the dean to remove me from the campus. This led to my taking a sabbatical from college life, and I performed in clubs and bars as the leader of a jazz trio. There I entered the "hard knocks school of life" and learned what no textbook could ever mention.

When I did return to the university to complete my education, I did so with a continuing appreciation and awareness of how much life is a theater offering us many opportunities for exploratory performance. I had acted as a musician and barroom entertainer, an amateur scientist, a preacher's kid, and as a rebellious student. The performative view prepared me to become a teacher who invited others to enter the theater of the classroom.

The Theater of Everyday Life

♣ Seeing life as theater helps you take yourself less seriously and develop an actor's appreciation and skill for flexible role assignments. With this flexibility, there is more room for experimentation and improvisation, enabling you to change how you act when the situation calls for your being different. Such flexibility is the key to moving out of stuck habits and roles which block the movement toward finding your path toward spirited living.

As performing actors we are able to prepare and even rehearse forthcoming scenes, alter them, redirect, and rewrite future showings. A performing life is always alive and open to the magic and creative energy of theater. Here grace and joy may be born through bringing more playfulness and levity into everyday matters, encouraging us to explore the unknown realms of eccentricity and absurd wisdom. As the early-twentieth-century artist Filippo Tommaso Marinetti expressed this invitation: "Let's break away from rationality as out of a horrible husk and throw ourselves like pride-spiced fruit into the immense, distorted mouth of the wind! Let's give ourselves up to the unknown, not out of desperation but to plumb the deep pits of the absurd."

When the wisdom of play is respected, we are able to be more creative and playful in every aspect of our daily life. As a therapist I have marveled at the devoted position a dog or cat may occupy in a family household. The lengths to which people will go to honor their pet is testimony enough of how natural it is for us to cultivate eccentricity. Our creatures are spoken and listened to, fed gourmet meals, provided a wardrobe, given imaginary histories, taken to their own therapist, buried in pet cemeteries, and occasionally show up in our dreams.

For families fortunate enough to have a rich pet life, I have occasionally suggested that they give their pet a special vacation. I ask them what it would be like to take a weekend and commit themselves to being servants of bliss to their pet. Would the dog like to be driven to a steakhouse and have a slab of beef, followed by a scented walk through a new park, and then topped by a heavenly nap atop a pile of lush pillows? In this way, the family is invited to design their own fantasy vacation for their pet. They are told to bring along a camera or videocamera and to keep an accurate record of every detail so that a scrapbook can be made.

No matter what condition the family is in, when they turn their attention to the adored pet and honor it with a special vacation, new vitality is brought into the family's life. They have an experience they will never forget, one that will unavoidably be filled with unbridled laughter, play, joy, and celebration. What they step into is pure living theater where the play requires serving their pet's delight. They become the playwright, director, actors, and audience to a production that may touch them in gentle and joyously absurd ways.

Life as art invites our spirited performance of it. Given the unpredictable nature of what confronts us, our participation in the theatrics of life becomes an invitation to improvise. Since we never know what anyone else will ever say or do at any given moment, we cannot rely exclusively upon previously designed lines, patter, and scripts. Although some spiritual and psychological orientations attempt to shape you into a predetermined form of conversation, experience, and story, every particular moment in life offers a unique opportunity for improvisation, invention, innovation, and change.

Doing Your Own Thing

❧ Improvisation invites you to creatively do your own thing. With this redefinition of life as a theatrical art of improvisation, we begin to see many of our traditional pathways in a different light. We are less inclined to debate what is the "most correct" style of spirituality.

The voices of different spiritual traditions are often persuasive in arguing that their approach is the most advanced, effective, true, ethical, or enlightening. Regard these voices of persuasion as the speaker's best effort to convince themselves that their way of living makes sense.

Soulful spirituality encourages you to listen more to your own voice and to draw upon your own resources. Never forget that teachers and texts may easily obscure the originating experiences that led to the text or institution. With this warning, be considerate of these suggestions:

1. Cultivate a healthy irreverence for all teachings (including this text).

2. Do what you want with any revered text, teaching, or idea—utilize it, ignore it, reverse it, distort it, and play with it from every angle.

3. Be cautious when it doesn't feel like play, and never forget that play is serious work.

4. It is possible for understanding to serve your spiritual evolution. With every new understanding, you become a different person—the person you previously were plus the new understanding. This new you cannot necessarily perform what worked for the previous you. This means you must always learn something different. Doing something different leads to a fresh experience, which in turn can bring forth a ripe understanding.

Beware of uncritically accepting the lines and scenes that others attempt to place you in. Consider how many adults return home to visit their parents and as soon as they pass through the front door they regress, interacting as they did in their adolescence. Similarly, mature, self-sufficient adults sometimes return to college and upon entering the classroom fall into the same helplessness they enacted when they were children in elementary school. Well-educated adults may also enter a religious institution and become blindly obedient to a religious leader in the same manner that they followed orders from their high school football coach.

Be particularly cautious about any privileged class of experts who are called "masters" or "gurus." To be regarded as a master is the first step toward unbecoming an imaginative and creative performer on

life's grand stage. Consider the consequences when others believe you
are a master. You will find that it no longer matters what you say. Everything uttered will be contextualized as a message from higher service.
A casual handshake will be taken as a sacred transmission of knowledge.
Personal stories about your childhood will be seen as holding secret messages. A belch becomes a brilliant teaching, and the snoring of a nap
will be regarded as the voice of spiritual wisdom. And all free-associative
blabberings of absolute nonsense will be carefully recorded as the spiritual discourse of the future. Beware the lies of fame.

Avoid the rigid posturings of "mastery" and return to embracing
and cultivating a beginner's mind. Maintain and respect your inborn
ignorance. Remember that crazy wisdom teaches us that we don't know
who, why, where, or what we are about. It is the master teacher of don't
know mind. Refrain from saying what you know. Speak to hear the surprise from your own theatrical voice.

Encourage yourself to adopt a more literary view of life. Read
less psychology and more literature. The finest works about human experience come from literature, not psychology. There is no better
demonstration of emotional paralysis than *Hamlet*. Literature and
drama help us encounter the multilayered, rich fabrics that hold human
experience and avoid the way in which psychology naively asserts that
complicated outcomes originate due to simple notions of billiard-ball
causality.

The composer John Cage once said that "theater takes place all
the time, wherever one is, and art simply facilitates persuading one that
this is the case." The art of spirited living involves appreciating, utilizing, and fully participating in the theater that holds our everyday experience.

Getting Tripped

❧ When our lives are shocked by unexpected outcomes, particularly those involving death and loss of loved ones, our everyday habits receive a jolt. I remember when I was thirteen years old and I ran up to the house filled with great delight to tell my family about the field trip I had been on. As soon as I opened the door, my dog burst forth to greet me and ran out onto the street where he was instantly killed by a passing car.

In a matter of seconds I went from the highest joy to the deepest sadness and was shocked by how my life had been so violently interrupted. That blow, in a very real sense, "blew my mind." It moved me into an altered state of consciousness where I was more susceptible to heartfelt emotions and more open and available to receiving spirit.

Years later when my grandfather died, I again felt my mind being blown by the impact of the news. At the moment his death was announced, time slowed down and my perception of the boundaries of my head began to shift. A stillness filled my mind, and I felt a tiny hole burst through the right rear side of my head. Slowly I experienced my mind being opened, emptied, and then filled with what sounded like a moving current of water.

We all have experiences that blow the limits of what our mind can understand or hold and find ourselves tripped into an alternative awareness. When this occurs, we may be tempted to seek the psychologies of repair as if they were a plumbing service and request that the hole be replugged. They give us explanations of our condition, often in terms of a stress response or traumatic reaction, and then assure us that we soon will be back in control. Alternatively, we can choose to live with this new opening into our mind and find that it is a lifeline to spirit. This is how the most difficult experiences of life bring a powerful spiritual gift. They trip us out of our habits of understanding and open us to receive spirit.

It is not only catastrophic life experience that opens you in this way. Anything that moves you out of your present habits may lead you to an experience that is outside of your expectations. After years of studying how people change their lives, I am still utterly amazed to realize how the tiniest change may initiate powerful processes of movement and personal development. When there is any alteration or interruption of your everyday patterns, habits, cycles, and rhythms, the potential for change is planted.

Changing the way you get to work, or the time of your meals, the music you listen to, the volume of your speech, the tempo of your walk, your gestures, or the way you watch television may set forth little snowballs that roll into an avalanche of change. Changes, no matter how small or quiet, typically produce nervous energy, as if your whole being reverberates with the recognition that a seed for ongoing change has been planted. As life becomes an experimental laboratory or theater for trying out different ways of altering your conduct, you become more able to discover and invent unique ways of moving yourself toward spirit.

All of the great teachers, healers, and spiritual guides I've met recognize that the art of teaching and making change involves helping arrange for an accident to happen. The accident is a way of tripping you out of your everyday routines. In this perspective, teaching has little or nothing to do with imparting information but is about helping trip another person to fall over and step beyond the limitations they have set for themselves.

Marpa, a twelfth-century Tibetan teacher, told his student Milarepa to construct a huge tower of stones. Milarepa spent years working on this and then Marpa instructed him to destroy it. Milarepa was stunned but tore it down anyway. He was furious and confused. As he knocked down the final stone, Marpa said, "Now look at your mind." At that moment he could see that his mind was no different from the tower he had built with his own hands, and that it could be brought down as easily as it was constructed. This realization could only have been conveyed through the ordeal of being tripped by his crazy wisdom teacher.

Our comfortable routines often hold us back from moving toward spirit. These habits are in a very real sense the expression of our everyday conventional mind, and it is this mind that needs to be opened and made available for more spontaneous and soulful expression. We tend to resist direct avenues to change ("Just stop doing it!") and are more easily drawn to diverting our flow ("Keep doing it, but do it in a different way."). Our whole being seems to want to preserve routines and habits and will thereby resist anything that looks like a direct challenge or threat to their survival. The surest way to change requires accepting the present routine, while making a change within or around it.

Playing with Crazy Wisdom

❧ One of the most powerful and effective ways of altering and undoing the routines of your life is to introduce some eccentricity, absurdity, and crazy wisdom. We already know that catastrophic experiences are experiential hurricanes whose arrival momentarily blows away all of our routines, and if we seize them as an opportunity for growth, we are blessed by them no matter how painful they initially are. Crazy wisdom is another powerful wind that also is capable of paralyzing and va-

porizing the routines of your everyday life. Taking a plunge into its absurdity will trip you over yourself in a way that brings about powerful
seeds for change while doing so with laughter and surprise rather than
tears.

When you find yourself being too serious, it is absolutely critical
that you change the playing field. For example, a stuck habit of overeat-
ing may invite you to explore some absurd things to do with your food.
Imagine singing to your food, perhaps by opening all of your kitchen
cabinets and refrigerator doors while serenading them with an improvised opera. Or dancing with your pasta and telling your ice cream a
joke. Doing anything absurd with your food helps get you out from
under the belief that dieting is all about resisting the desire to overeat.
The habits of your everyday life call you to practice crazy wisdom and
bring about the don't know mind.

If a couple feels stuck in their relationship and attempts to have
a serious conversation to sort matters out, it is likely that they will feel
more stuck. They are already drowning in being too serious about
themselves, and the more serious they become, the more closed they
are to the creative and imaginative processes that are needed to get them
unstuck. It could be as simple as having them call a marital counselor
and asking whether they sell any free love, or calling a church or synagogue and asking the clergy whether they believe God is present at their
wedding ceremonies. Or they may have to go to a restaurant and order
a main course they both dislike and then have it boxed up, taken home,
and thrown away, followed by an absolutely wild culinary fling with a
desert they both love.

Take the absurdity of crazy wisdom and the crazy wisdom of absurdity with more seriousness than you ever have before. The spirit of
a child dances at the thought of watching the world in a novel and crazy
way. Unless we can open ourselves to that Forrest Gumpish mind of

playfulness, it is likely that the doors to soulful spirituality are going to remain too rusted to swing open. To find everyday soul you must give birth to more mirth.

Taking Yourself Less Seriously

♣ We live in a world of experience that is more slippery and literary than it is concrete and statistical. As William Blake once framed it, "Do what you will, this Life's a Fiction and is made up of Contradiction." There is no way to logically figure out why you are here and why you should bother asking. We live in so many contradictory truths that only a work of fiction is able to reveal the paradoxical and often contradictory truths of our situation.

Anyone, whether they are a psychologist, theologian, teacher, or otherwise, who claims they can help you fully understand yourself is intoxicated with overseriousness.

There is no better place to begin than spending some time in front of a mirror looking as ridiculous as you possibly can. Make weird faces, do absolutely nutty things to your hair, use makeup in the wrong way, dress inappropriately, and closely observe how easy it is to make yourself look like an idiot.

The more advanced form of this tactic requires inviting a friend or a group of friends to spend an afternoon together taking photographs that are an exposé on lunacy. The goal is to create many ridiculous photographs of each other. The sillier, the better. The photo album that results helps you in the future when you catch yourself being too serious about life.

As part of this photo album, write an obituary for your seriousness, noting the day that seriousness passed away, and give some spe-

cific recollections of how it once lived. Colleagues, friends, and relatives who were closest to your seriousness are acknowledged, and then
the obituary is typed and sent to those who made the album with you.
At least one day a year is set aside to have an annual celebration of the
time you all decided to live with less seriousness.

There are many ways to perform the absence of seriousness that
frees you to laugh at yourself and the importance of never taking yourself too seriously again. In these ways we exercise our don't know mind
and help prepare the ground for a spirited life.

Revere Your Errors

✦ The musician Brian Eno developed what he called "Oblique Strategies," referring to ways of directing himself outside of his routine habits
and down the side roads that bring new experiences. The first strategy
he ever wrote was, "Honor thy error as a hidden intention." In other
words, there are unspoken teachings, guidings, and intentions within
you that are communicated through the indirect pathway of throwing
an error, mistake, or accident into your daily conduct. When we goof
up, we should pause and ask ourselves whether our deepest being is trying to tell us something.

Learn to respect unexpected mistakes that take place in your conduct. Keep a record of them. Study your mistakes as if they were a secret code that can be broken, revealing deeper secrets about your hidden
talents and desires.

This awareness helps our errors become the seeds for more interesting futures than the one we habitually envision. Use your mistakes
as teachers that point to new ways of evolving your participation in the
theater of life. All absurd enactments help bring forth unexpected outcomes, enabling us to go into a future we never would have otherwise

entered. As a spiritual practice, it enables us to trip ourselves right into the heart and soul of life's merriment.

Holy Fools

✷ Black Elk, the great Oglala Sioux Holy Man, proclaimed that outside of tears, truth comes to us through the voice of laughter. Humor brings forth truths that can not be known through any other means. Many different spiritual traditions give special importance to the contributions of the sacred fool, holy jester, and trickster. Humor not only conveys what otherwise could not be heard, it helps balance the overly serious experiences of life and helps restore you to a more centered place.

Called *heyoka* by the Sioux, *chaazhini* by the Navajo, *koshare* by the Zia and Acoma Pueblo, *koyemsi* by the Zuni, sacred fools shock onlookers with their unpredictability. Whether they are flirting during a solemn ceremony, laughing at a funeral, or weeping at a joke, everyone understands that they have accepted the very important responsibility of helping keep everything in balance through their contrary conduct.

The human mind, to quote Jane Wagner, is like a piñata, and "when it breaks open, there're a lot of surprises inside. Once you get the piñata perspective, you see that losing your mind can be a peak experience." Crazy wisdom shows us the empty, don't know mind that the spirit calls home.

Whether it be a natural catastrophe or an unnatural absurdity, life brings many different ways of tripping us over ourselves. We need to stop running away from these fallings and begin seeing their value and contribution to our spiritual journey. We don't have to worry about whether the natural catastrophes will come. We will each receive a full share of these, including the inevitability of our own death and the passing on of everyone we love.

But we can do something about bringing forth the truths that are carried by absurd experience and crazy wisdom. We can learn to be more eccentric and absurd in our everyday life and see these moments as sacred. As we cultivate the deep practice of tripping ourselves, strong connections to spirit will emerge.

Becoming a True Character in the Theater of Life

♣ I am the only me and you are the only you. Begin paying more attention to people who have found interesting ways of expressing their uniqueness. They most likely discovered their unique way of being in the world by experimenting with a wide variety of roles, lines, and scripts until they found how to move beyond the role of being "normal." They escaped the dis-ease of normality by getting over their stereotyped self.

Every actor dreams of finding the part that will make their career. In a similar fashion, each of us awaits the part or the role that will bring out our best. The only way to find this truth is to step onto your spirited stage and start the play, knowing that with a passionate and compassionate commitment to improvisation your way will be found.

EXERCISE ONE

Using Nonsense to Help Free You from Over-Understanding

♣ One of the most powerful ways to free yourself from the closed mindedness of over-understanding and overseriousness is to flood your mind with nonsense. The general understandings shared by the cultural community are often the very understandings that impede our movement toward soulful spirituality. For instance, according to the advice proposed by educational institutions, you must have a high school diploma or college degree before you can say that you are "prepared for life." More generally speaking, this sense dictates the seldom challenged assumption that you must be an expert to do anything. This results in the fragmentation of everyday life, where the idealized lifestyle is defined as someone who has a chef prepare the meals, an accountant take care of the bills, a hair designer comb your hair, a fitness expert take over your exercise program, a hypnotist put you to sleep, and a psychoanalyst interpret your dreams.

In our culture, we breed a fantasy that expertise can make everything right. Psychotherapists prove that they have this understanding by passing an examination consisting of multiple-choice questions regarding the technical vocabulary and theories of psychology. Similarly, lawyers must pass the bar exam and doctors take a written test to prove that they hold the necessary understanding to be called an expert in their profession.

Upon closer examination, these procedures of legitimatizing expertise aren't always that sensible. What does giving a right answer on a quiz have to do with helping another person, whether in psychotherapy, medicine, or law? It may be completely irrelevant or even problematic. When I refer someone to a therapist, I want them to see someone who can relate to their particular situation and design a therapeutic experience that is unique to their needs. To be able to work in this individualized way requires abandoning the kind of simplistic generalizations that a psychological licensing examination is concerned with. It has more to do with their being able to serve another person through the creative and resourceful use of their whole being. From the spiritual perspective, true expertise flows from a don't know mind rather than a know-it-all mind. Even Albert Einstein confessed that he had learned physics in spite of his education.

Begin by making yourself a special diploma saying that you have been granted a Doctorate of Philosophy in Not Knowing. As you prepare yourself to make this diploma, remind yourself again that the spiritual elders and revered teachers throughout all of history have told us that enlightenment comes to a don't know mind, not one filled with education. Neither Jesus, Abraham, Buddha, or Mohammed had a college degree, diploma, nor professional license to teach, heal, counsel, or guide others. They fulfilled their destiny through emptying their minds of what was held as conventional sense and surrendering their lives to a spiritual experience.

Each of us enters the world with our Doctorate of Philosophy in Not Knowing. To remind yourself of the expertise you were granted at birth, award yourself the appropriate diploma and place it somewhere to remind you that you already know that you don't know and that is what you need to know the most. In this emptiness of a true beginner's mind, all that you need can come when it is time for it to be present.

You can also make diplomas in a Certificate of Silence, License to Be Still, Postgraduate Training in Being, and Professor Emeritus of Emptiness, or whatever comes to you as an expression of what is most essential to our life as spiritual beings but can not be earned at any institution because it is given free at birth.

Once you have rewarded yourself with one of these special diplomas, proceed to sabotage any disturbing, culturally prescribed understanding in the following way. Carry some cards of nonsense with you at all times. Here are some examples to get you started:

- Today is the yes of yesterday.
- Humor is both a barking dog and a clapping hand.
- If you don't know, you know.

Begin a collection of these sayings and carry several with you each day. There are books of humorous reflections that you should feel free to draw upon. Some of my favorites include:

"All 'isms' should be 'wasms.' " (Abbie Hoffman)

"God has no religion." (Mahatma Gandhi)

"He has observ'd the Golden Rule Till he's become the
     Golden Fool." (William Blake)

"Only the shallow know themselves." (Oscar Wilde)

Whenever you catch yourself struggling with a difficulty in your life, immediately reach for a card that holds one of these uncommon sayings and read it. A little dose of crazy wisdom is often what is needed to release us from the grip of a problem.

EXERCISE TWO

Fooling Around with Your Least Important Routines

♣ Make a personal inventory of your everyday routines and determine which ones are the least important. Do they include taking out the trash, dusting your furniture, reading junk mail, throwing your pen into the air and catching it, placing your dirty clothes in a special place, filling your car with gas, purchasing a soft drink, taking the dog for a walk, or removing lint from your clothes? When you have identified several of these routines, make some plans to tinker, experiment, and fool around with them in order to help bring forth some surprise and wonder.

If you choose the routine of taking out the trash, consider how you can alter this activity. You could change the time you do it, per-haps shifting it from being a morning task to being a late-evening out-ing. Or you could alter the place where you keep the trash, or make a difference in how you carry it, release it, look at it, think about it, and feel about it. What if you recited a special limerick to your trash before throwing it away or gave it a parting gift? Imagine asking your trash if it had any last request before it left your house and then allow yourself to free-associate on what it might say if it were able to talk. Would it ask to have another night inside the house or be fed a final meal?

As you fool around with your least important routines, begin seeing this as a safe laboratory for finding ways of introducing more and crazy wisdom into your life. Begin wondering whether these least important routines will someday become more important because of the freshness you now are bringing to them. How could taking out the trash become a ceremonial act that helps you enter a sacred space? Would it require changing your trash can into an altar for objects that are passing on to a new life? Would you start blessing your trash and thanking it for what it brought you?

These questions and orientations help bring an absurd hint of mystery and wonder into your everyday life. The secrets of spirituality are not necessarily revealed through entering golden or pearly gates. When the ordinary is transformed into the extraordinary, we bring a sense of wonder and enchantment into the world.

EXERCISE THREE

Have a Dinner Conversation
Where No One Tells the Truth

♣ Have a conversation that carries you into the wildest flights of fantasy regarding past experiences and spiritual pilgrimages. One of the best ways to accomplish this is to have dinner with another person and agree to not tell the truth to one another.

You may do this with someone you know, but also consider doing it with someone you are not yet well acquainted with. When I work with groups, I will give this task as their first assignment before they have gotten to know one another. Sometimes I request that they never tell anything true about themselves for the entire weekend we are working together. All utterances about their past and present must be fictional accounts.

What takes place is often quite remarkable. People are more likely to express their deepest desires, dreams, and unconscious longings when they try making it up. In this sense, their lies reveal more profound truths about their life than anything that would be uttered in an effort to be purposefully true. When you discover that your lie is more true to your self than your truth, that realization chips away at the reliability of your conscious efforts to understand your life. It leaves you less confident in controlling your life and more trustful of stopping, stilling, emptying.

As you contemplate how dinners that try to avoid the truth may become an agent of soulful change, reflect on the ways in which you actually lie when you try to tell the truth to another person. If you are not in touch with your fantasies and are not giving a voice to your imagination, is this in some deep sense a lie? The line between truth and fiction is not as clear as it may seem. Sometimes truth can only be known in fiction, and this is often the case when we approach the situation of being human and in our movement toward a spiritual life.

EXERCISE FOUR

Spiritual First-Aid Kit: Antidotes for Closed Minds

❦ Make plans to put together your own spiritual first-aid kit. Fill it with these items: a small feather; a miniature toy animal; and a collection of absurd quotations. The small feather should be the most sacred-looking feather you can find while the toy animal should be the creature that you believe is most symbolic of humor. Keep these items wrapped up in a small box labeled "Spiritual First-Aid Kit."

The last item for your kit is a collection of crazy-wisdom quotations. Each should be written on a tiny piece of paper; they may be taken from quotation books or freshly made by your own literary inventiveness. Here are some that could be included:

> "You may never get to touch the Master, but you can tickle
> his creatures."
> (Thomas Pynchon)

> Start a huge, foolish project,
> like Noah.
> It makes absolutely no difference,
> what people think of you."
> (Rumi)

> "Zen is not letting yourself be horsewhipped into words
> about it,
> so as you read these words, just unfocus your eyes and
> stare at the blurry page."
> (Jack Kerouac)

The next time you find your mind or emotions too tightly closed, go to your spiritual first-aid kit. Carefully remove its contents and hold the miniature animal while readying yourself to tickle its belly with the feather. After selecting an absurd quotation, read it outloud to your creature, then tickle its belly. Try not to laugh at the pomp with which you perform your emergency treatment.

Experiment with different feathers and toy animals until you find the ones that tickle you the most. Keep on the lookout for new quotations that will provide fresh medicines for your kit. You may also use this procedure as a means of preventive medicine so that it helps keep your mind open to the unexpected ways in which being tripped by the absurd helps prepare you for soulful spirituality.

There are spiritual teachings that advise us to regard all appearances as illusion, as a lie that hides the inner truth that cannot be viewed through habitual seeing. Regarding everything we comfortably know as a deception suggests that we find a way to trip over the familiar. How are we to rid ourselves of our habits and step into a fresh way of being in the world?

Spiritual teachers suggest that the way out involves acting on what we already know and believe. We must enact our deepest habits and escalate them until they collapse. In other words, we don't necessarily have to take anything away from our inner "towers of Babel," but we can add to them until they are so top-heavy that they collapse. They exaggerate, escalate, make ridiculous, and topple what we regard as unmovable.

In the Feast of Fools we join all of our assumptions and beliefs and carry them to their illogical end. William Blake's idea that "the fool who persists in his folly will become wise" points to this strategy of liberation. Rather than resist a problem, such as the idea that one has insomnia, we are encouraged to experiment with it. If you believe you suffer from this sleep disorder, it won't help to be told that it is possible to get a good night's sleep if you simply relax. Trying not to sleep may accidentally free you from it. In this way, you play with the assumption of its truth in order to prove its falsity.

When we realize that life involves one trip after another, we find a pulse and beat to its motion. In jazz it is the beat or the rhythm that moves the music forward, but what brings the energy and life force of soul is found in the way the beat surprises us. Syncopation, the way we accentuate the unexpected, is the special ingredient needed to bring out the rhythmic swing we recognize as soul. Give some spirited importance to the unnoticed activities of your life, whether they be taking out the trash or bathing your pet, and see these new accents as ways of syncopating your everyday with soul. Looking at taking out the trash as a sacred act is a moment of soulful syncopation.

Walker Percy observed that tourists find it practically impossible to really see the Grand Canyon, that is, see it with the same sense of surprise and wonder that gripped García López de Cárdenas when, after crossing the desert, he peered through the mesquite and stood before it. We see it through the eyes of familiarity and expectation, laid out by the photographs and postcards that have been etched into our consciousness.

To have a chance to see it with fresh eyes might require a catastrophe. An earthquake would work just fine if it left us dangling on a new edge where we looked out and saw it with naked eyes for the first time. Another way suggested by Percy is to avoid all familiar pathways that have been built for you to see the canyon. Camping in the backcountry, staying clear of all trails and lookout points might open the canyon to being seen if you were lucky enough to accidentally find it.

Crazy wisdom is all about tripping us into the surprises of spirit. It sets us up to have an accident of enlightenment. It is the poet and the muse of our soul and its voice invites us to enter the open field of a beginner's mind, the mind that knows that it does not know. As D. H. Lawrence reminds us, "Man fixes some wonderful erection of his own between himself and the wild chaos, and gradually goes bleached and stifled under his parasol. Then comes a poet, enemy of convention, and makes a slit in the umbrella; and lo! the glimpse of chaos is a vision, a window to the sun."

2 ❧ *Lifelines to Spirit*

CHAPTER FOUR

❧

Being in Rhythm: The Opening of the Heart

As the World Tree stands at the center of the vast planes of the cosmos, song stands at the intimate center of the cosmos of the individual. At that moment when the shaman song emerges, when the sacred breath rises up from the depths of the heart, the center is found, and the source of all that is divine has been tapped.

—JOAN HALIFAX

*I*T IS SUNDAY morning at the New Salem Missionary Baptist Church, located in the heart of the Minneapolis African-American community. Although I am the only white man in the congregation, I feel completely welcomed and accepted by the church mothers and fathers, as their elders are affectionately called. "Give me a hug, Brother Brad," Alice says as the pastor's mother greets me with open arms and the loving touch of her soft and mature hands. Every week is a family reunion at New Salem as well as a holy time to invite the spirit into the hearts of all who come.

The organist, a young man in his early twenties, takes his seat and begins playing a few soulful bars of music, announcing the rhythms that will soon commence. As he does this, the drummer and other musicians, dressed like professional entertainers, set up their instruments while everyone awaits the energetic explosion. The drums soon begin and the choir claps their hands, moving down the aisle to the front of the church.

The deacons now step out and take their place facing the congregation. Led by Brother Amos and Brother Roy, they shout out prayers and lead us in hymns and chants, "Jesus Is on the Mainline," "Precious Lord," and "This Little Light of Mine, I'm Gonna Let It Shine." In the midst of this celebration many stand when the spiritual current moves them to do so. All this takes place as the beat is syncopated with hand-clapping, providing a thunderous counterpoint to the drummer's pulse.

During the choir's singing and in the midst of the chanted prayers, parishioners periodically join in with cries of "Amen!" "Uh-huh!" "Thank you, thank you!" or "Say it!" As the deacons finish orchestrating our prayer and song, the preacher, Reverend Jerry McAfee, a former professional singer and one-time street preacher in Los Angeles, steps to the podium and invites everyone to lift the intensity even higher.

His sermon quickly turns into a vigorous singsong chant that is perfectly delivered to escalate and widen the pervasive mood of sanctified ecstasy. As Reverend McAfee's chanting intensifies, the organ and drummer punctuate it with loud staccato chords and rhythmic bursts of percussion. The congregation responds with short shouts during the breaks in his vigorous cadence. The volume and pitch continue to rise until the organ and musicians break open into a song that invites clapping, jumping, shaking, and dancing.

When you are in the midst of an authentic African-American church service like those held at the New Salem Missionary Baptist Church, you have no doubt that it is the kind of church experience that

Zora Neale Hurston regarded as a pure continuation of the ceremonial drumming, dancing, and music that takes place in Africa. It is a dramatic performance of spirit-making that brings ecstatic soul to all the bodies it moves. In this sanctuary of rhythm, the beat of soul is everywhere—in sung rhythms, hummed rhythms, spoken rhythms, hand-clapping, foot-patting, dancing legs and arms, drum beats, tambourine swishes, cymbal crashes, and the percussive chords of the blazing organ. Soul is perpetually reborn and moved into the lives of its spiritual practitioners through rhythm.

The African-American church is the birthplace of soulful music in our culture. It originated the beat that enabled Ray Charles to become the "High Priest of Soul" during the fifties, and it is where a whole movement of music found its roots. Whether it was voiced by Aretha Franklin, Les McCann, or Cyrus Chestnut, soul was deeply engrained within the global musical scene by those who grew up with gospel in their community church.

As an adult I was baptized in this soulful spirit. There the rhythms of clapping hands, beating drums, swaying bodies, and inspired music and prayers opened my heart and returned me to the currents of spirit I had felt as a young boy in the churches of my father and grandfather.

A warm luminescence fills the church when it is blessed by the congregation's sincere praying and worship. You can actually see this white light and feel it coming into your heart. The joy that touches you is not the simple excitement associated with being pleased by something you like. It is a tearful realization of sacred clarity. An electric sensation ripples through your body and your inner being glows.

In the church I was able to feel the inseparable union, the yoke of the world's suffering with its peace and joy. As illogical as it may seem, in the light of spirit you know that you cannot run away from suffering. It's like being around the wind of a hurricane. If you run toward its periphery, you will be blown to pieces. But if you stop trying to run away from it and walk into its center, you will find the eye of the storm, a place of great calm and peace.

The currents of spirit in this inner-city church were like this: People brought their pain and openly cried out for mercy. Men and women who had been through multiple treatments for severe drug addictions were at the end of their line, and they came to completely give their lives to the spirit that was alive in their church. Every week brought violence to some church family, sometimes the death of an adolescent or child caused by the random assault of a gang shooting. There were parishioners who had no food for their table, no money to pay for heat in the winter, no transportation, and no access to necessary medical care. With these life-challenging ordeals, they went to church to pray for grace and mercy. They came to face and enter the difficult storms of their lives and to find the spiritual center where peace awaited. Without the storm, there could be no eye of calm.

One woman in the community, now a member of the Grammy Award–winning group, Sounds of Blackness, had dreamed of a large piano keyboard where Jesus walked her over the keys. When she awakened, she was amazed to find that she had learned how to play a new song on the piano, even though she did not know how to play before.

Practitioners of the African-American traditional church believe that any kind of musical experience is possible for those filled with spirit, and historians are well aware that many of their songs were born spontaneously in the midst of a spirited service. Take this church newsletter account of a young African-American woman who, on April 9, 1906, had her first experience with this kind of music making:

"I sang under the power of the Spirit in many languages, the interpretation both of words and music I had never before heard, and in the home where the meeting was held, the Spirit led me to the piano, where I played and sang under inspiration, although I had not learned to play."

In music and rhythm, the spirit may enter and "give sweeter songs than lips can sing." This experience is not limited to solo performances. It is also capable of moving a whole congregation to sing spontaneous choral arrangements. Sometimes called "tongue-singing," a reference to "speaking with the tongues of angels" (glossolalia), it is like a wave of sound that comes over the entire group with everyone singing in perfect celestial harmony.

Soulful music is not made by musicians, it moves through them. The music arises spontaneously from the deepest rhythms of their souls and moves the voice, keyboard, and instrument to resonate with it. As an old-time evangelist once put it, "Not everybody can sing with the voice, but everybody can have a whole music-box deep down in the soul."

Here we learn that soul is not an abstract psychological or religious concept but a way of feeling the rhythm of life itself. When music has a vital beat, we say that it has soul. Life has soul when we feel a beat that makes us want to move and dance. "It don't mean a thing if it ain't got that swing" is all you need to know about soul, whether in music or everyday life.

The Rhythms of Soul Will Always Include Bliss and Suffering

♣ We too often ignore the way life presents itself as an ever-changing and ever-pulsing rhythmic dance. Moments of happiness fade away, and when suffering enters the stage we feel cheated, disappointed, and even guilty. Like the weather, our everyday emotions and experiences will change if we simply wait a while. No one has a problem or symptom that is present as a steady state twenty-four hours a day. And no one is happy and peaceful twenty-four hours a day. The experience of suffering has its own rhythm and goes back and forth upon the stage of our experience.

We commit all sorts of foolishness when we think that we can hold on to bliss forever or be completely free of suffering. We must dance with the rhythms of life. Dave Gehue, a Micmac medicine man from Nova Scotia, described to me his relationship with spirituality as simply one of "going along for the ride." When we mount the rhythms of spirit, we should allow the horse to take us where it wants to go. This is the essence of moving with and being moved by a spirited life.

Music flows naturally when you move with the rhythms that hold it. Jazz musicians who have learned to stop trying to make the music, and instead prepare themselves to be moved by the music, find that it will flow so naturally and effortlessly that it may become difficult to shut it off. When the rhythms naturally move through, the idea of right and wrong notes is dissipated. As any devoted listener to music can tell you, listening to someone play all the right notes without heart and soul is music that is wrong. On the other hand, playing the wrong notes with heart and soul sounds musically right.

Life Is Rhythm

✤ One of the oldest spiritual practices and one of the quickest ways to discover rhythm is to meditate on the breath. The important lesson to be learned from meditation has little to do with being a masterful observer of your own breath but takes place when you truly learn to become the rhythm of breathing. The in and out of breathing is a pulse and a rhythm that creates, holds, manifests, and comprises life itself.

To see breath is one thing, but to surrender and fully fall into the rhythm is to realize soul.

Becoming the rhythm of breath is not an easy accomplishment. Our minds habitually wander when we try to be still, and we find that it is difficult to have an undivided focus upon that which is most critical for sustaining our life—our breath. We too easily step outside of a full realization of our breath and begin observing and critiquing it, or we make hypotheses and theories about our life, or predictions of where we may go, or replay past memories and experiences.

Again, our mind is like the rider of a horse who pays little or no attention to where the horse wants to go. We hold on so tightly to the reins that all we are aware of is the tension in our hands and we don't feel the horse's movement. In the practice of meditation we must learn to relax our grip, drop the reins, feel the horse, and become one with its movement. When this takes place, there is no awareness of any difference between the horse and its rider. There is only the rhythm of movement. This is what is meant by becoming the rhythm of your breath. It is an awakening of spirit through becoming inseparable from the soulful rhythms of life.

Everything in life is held together by rhythm. Anthropologist Edward Hall had graduate students take a hidden camera to film a group of children while they played during the school lunch hour. When the film was first examined, the children looked like they were each doing their own thing, some running, others skipping, and so forth. Hall invited his students to observe the film at different speeds while holding the belief that the whole group was connected through some pattern, rhythm, or social choreography.

Gradually the entire group was seen as moving to a definite rhythm that followed a particularly active child who seemed to be directing the beat. With the help of a rock musician, they found some music that fit the social rhythm. When the music was synchronized with the children's movements, it appeared that the children were actually dancing to it. From such studies, Hall concluded that "people in interactions move together in a kind of dance, but they are not aware of their synchronous movement and they do it without music or conscious orchestration."

There is rhythm and dance in every breath that we take, in our interactions with others, and in every aspect of our lives. Our conversations shift in the movements between talking and listening, our feelings for one another breathe up and down, as do the tides of our hope and despair. Everything in our life is moving and displaying the pulse of rhythm. Becoming more aware of these rhythms, falling into them, and being more deeply moved by them brings soul into our everyday life.

We easily become stuck in the lyrics of psychology and lose connection to the music and rhythm of spirituality when we give too much importance to a single label or understanding of our life. If you believe that you are an "introverted, intuitive overachiever," then you may use this simplistic categorization of yourself to explain the whole of your being. Unfortunately, it does more than explain your life. It limits you to performing what your definition says you are capable of doing.

What if you developed a rare cognitive condition where you could not recognize or understand the words people were saying but could hear the tonality, rhythm, and music within their speech? You might find that you are able to have a clearer sense of what the other person is communicating, even though you have no ability to identify their words.

As we learn to hear and feel the world's rhythms, we forget ourselves and fall into the dance of life. We learn what indigenous elders never forget. Completely in tune with the rhythms of their natural surroundings, they know where the food is at each season of the year.

Among the Aborigines of Australia, finding food comes from knowing that there is a rhythm, a time and place for everything. Through spending many hours watching and listening to animals, they learn to imitate their movements, sounds, and rhythms. When they perform a ceremonial dance prior to a hunt, the rhythms of the animal they are hunting enters their being as they dance its movements and sing its song. This enables them to be in step with the movement of their prey so they are present at the right place and time. Being in tune with the music and rhythms of the bush is the key to finding what they need to survive.

To See Differently, Move Differently

♣ Everything that lives does so within the rhythm of life. Nothing is alive that isn't organized by a pulsing motion or the rhythmic dancing of its internal components and processes. Whether it be the moving tides of our bloodstream, the percussion of our heart, or the motion of our bodies, we are filled with rhythms and movement.

Even our eyes constantly make fast movements so as to keep different images upon our retina. If the images stop changing and become one stabilized image, what we are looking at will fade and disappear. Our eyes must literally pulse and dance with the world in order to see it in a stable way.

What we see and hear is determined by the way we choreograph our relationship with the world. When you change this dance, you alter what you see. The early American experimental psychologist G. M. Stratton invented special eyeglasses that used mirror systems to alter retinal images and turned what the viewer saw upside down. After wearing these glasses for several days, Stratton was amazed to find that everything he observed became "normal." He could even walk with ease.

However, when he removed the eyeglasses he had become accustomed to wearing, the world again became bewildering. He had to relearn how to see what others regarded as "undistorted," but which had now become "distorted" to his new way of seeing.

Artists are sometimes more appreciative of the time needed for a person to learn how to move or change themselves so that they see the world in a new and different way. In addressing a complaint that his portrait of Gertrude Stein did not look like her, Picasso replied, "Never mind, it will."

Similarly, the actions necessary to see the world of soulful spirituality may take us through a period of disorientation and confusion while we learn to move with it. Some orientations to body work such as the Alexander method follow a similar process. They move your body into different postures and positions so that you can experience yourself in a different space, one that is more aligned and balanced. When you leave the office you eventually return to your old habits of body movement, but this time you feel uncomfortable because your body remembers what it felt like to be properly aligned and balanced. Your body then starts moving itself and searching for the previous state of alignment. This initiates a period of transition where you hang between being uncomfortable with an old habit while longing for the balanced state that was once momentarily experienced.

This same transitional process holds for spirituality. When we are touched by spirit, whether in a powerful prayer meeting, an ecstatic ceremony, or in moments of illumination, we experience what it is like to be spiritually tuned. As we fall back into old habits, we immediately feel a discomfort and longing for the spirit that previously awakened us into a new awareness and sense of well-being. Our lives search for a practice or path that will help us return home to its balancing touch. This is when we must remember that the transition requires perseverance, patience, and trust. As you wait to remount the spiritual horse, you trust that there is a movement that will come and dance you into the heart of spirited living.

Drumming Yourself into Soul

✶ Snares, tom-toms, cymbals, gongs, damarus, surdo, berimbau, rattles, stampers, clappers, scrapers, kettledrums, barrel drums, frame drums, tabla, marimba, steel drums, bass drums, water drums, blocks, and bells provide us with many ways to experiment with making rhythm. Thanks to Mickey Hart's superb book, *Drumming at the Edge of Magic: A Journey into the Spirit of Percussion,* and the many recordings, performances, and workshops on drumming that have taken place, we have learned more about how rhythm carries people into the belly of the spiritual fire.

Practically all indigenous cultures value the importance of a drum for helping bring forth a spirited ceremony. I was taken to a village in South Africa to meet an elder healer called the Mother Sangoma. She brought out four huge drums made of metal ketals, which were covered with elephant skins. As the drums were played in her small ceremonial hut, the sound became a thunderous energy that caused my whole body to pulse.

It was not possible to sit still and listen. The energy of the drum was playing my own skin and internal organs to the extent that I lost my ability to maintain conscious control of my experience. My body spontaneously moved into dance, and as I sat on top of this drumming energy, it rode me into the spirit world. I recognized it as the same pulse that swayed the bodies in the Sunday morning service of the African-American church, and I again experienced firsthand how drumming the rhythms of soul is the oldest way to open ourselves to being danced by spirit.

Bringing in the Rhythm

✤ The soul is not an "it" that we really are looking for but a rhythm that must be danced with. In fact, it is less dancing with the rhythm of life than being danced by the rhythm. Surrendering to the rhythms of your everyday life is the beginning, middle, and end of your spirited journey. There you will find the spiritual current that moves your life into the tides of soulful expression.

Recognize the rhythms in your life and find ways to be more in synch with them. Notice the rhythms of energy and tiredness that take place within you and orchestrate your life to flow with them, whether it be adding a nap or altering your sleep schedule. Pay attention to the rhythms of your spouse's or partner's speech. Give them the space to exercise their rhythms and find ways to dance harmoniously with it. How often do you need to be still? Create a lifestyle rhythm that can accommodate a time for your stillness, as well as your play and work activities.

Look outside of yourself to the rhythms that surround you. Learn the cycles and rhythms of your local weather, even the animals, trees, plants, birds, and insects that live around you. The Cree medicine man Albert Lighting taught that our inner nature and rhythms are an exact copy of the universe. When we become unaware of the rhythms that are inside and outside of ourselves, we feel out of kilter with life. Medicine people recognize that there is a right time and place for everything and their job is to get you into the rhythm that brings forth the pulse of healing. Albert once said, "Someone practicing good medicine never does so by personally summoning supernatural powers. He or she is simply told ahead of time what is going to happen and then helps it happen." In other words, they tune into the rhythms of life and recognize when and where the beat will fall.

If you are out of synch with life's rhythms, you will feel out of step with your own being. If you are in step and fully synchronous with the rhythms that embrace you, your life will be filled with the mysteries of synchronicity and soulful presence. What you need to hear, see, and feel will be present when it is needed, creating an almost magical sense that your life is in the groove it was born to find.

Falling into this rhythm has less to do with know-how, understanding, or expertise. It has more to do with trust. As an old and wise deacon of an inner-city church once told me, "Stop trying to lead life and allow yourself to be led one step at a time." Life is holding you in its dance. It is your partner. Feel its lead as it waits to move you into its mystery, wonder, and enchantment.

EXERCISE ONE

Finding the Rhythm of Your Breath

✣ If you are a meditator, then pretend for a moment that you have never meditated. If you have never meditated, then consider yourself fortunate that you may enter into this exercise with a fresh beginner's mind. I want to invite you to meditate in a way that is free from all complications and teachings. It is simply a way of having an awareness of your breath as a rhythm of life. You may do this by arranging for a special time to be still, or while taking a walk, or while you're waiting somewhere.

It may be done anywhere and at anytime, but with one recommendation. When you start this practice, do it no more than one minute at a time. You may repeat it as many times as you wish during the course of a day, but try not to do it longer than a minute. As you become more skilled with this practice, you may advance to three or four minutes, but you really don't need more than five minutes. A short period of time will allow you to fully focus on the task which will make it a brief but powerful intervention into your everyday activities.

This meditation asks that you imagine a drumming or percussive sound that accompanies the pulse of your own breath. This rhythm may be as simple as a ballroom waltz or country two-step, complex as an experimental symphony, or in any style ranging from rock to rap to classical to jazz. Decide whether the bottom of your exhaled breath will be heard as the deep thud of a bass drum or as a cymbal crash or tympani roll. Similarly, create an imagined sound for hitting the peak of inhalation. With these sounds that mark the incoming and outgoing peaks of breathing, proceed to fill the space in between them with whatever improvised rhythms enter your imagination. You might periodically choose to be a metronome, while at other times performing a hypnotic samba or bossa nova. Allow the life situation you're in at the time of the exercise to shape the rhythm that is most fitting, whether it be a loud march or soft brush work on a finely tuned snare drum.

Concentrate so that your whole being is making rhythms that flow within the pulse of your breath. As you attend to falling into these beats, your mind will be stilled from internal chatter. This meditation will help you fall more deeply in touch with the natural rhythms of your own breathing and will help you find the beat of soul.

As you play your own internal drums, see over the course of time whether there are particular rhythms that come to you. Each of us carries our own beats and rhythms. Commit yourself to this meditative practice as a means of finding your own rhythms, the beat that lives within the beat of your every breath. When you are certain that you have found one of these rhythms, record yourself playing it upon a solid surface.

When you are satisfied with a particular recording, play it for a meditation session. Allow your breath to get into synch with it. Now add an accompanying rhythm inside your mind as a means of bringing forth a deeper rhythm, a beat that lies within the one you have already brought into the external world. Practice weaving rhythms into those rhythms that, due to your practice, have become familiar and habitual to you. Begin to appreciate that bringing one rhythm into another rhythm is a form of dance and that you are learning new ways of dancing with yourself.

As rhythm becomes a larger part of your life and clearly marks the essence of your meditative practice, allow your inner voice to add some music. Every meditative session will now have music that moves with the beat. Allow your voice to be internally heard as any musical instrument or ensemble you desire and free it to be completely improvisational. Familiar songs may be voiced, or completely improvised lines of music may be invented. Give no thought to making this music, but allow it to naturally come forth. Do not require that your music fit any familiar form. It may be one tone that occasionally expresses itself or it may become a shower of tones that could never be repeated again due to its complexity and unfamiliarity.

The word "spirit" is from the Latin *spiritus,* the word for "breath," and for some indigenous people, such as the Klamath Indians, it is also related to the word for song. This insight helps us realize that spirit is a breathing of song and that music is the breath of spirit. It follows that medicine men and women as well as other mystics have entered the realm of the divine through singing a special song given to them in moments of profound ecstasy.

EXERCISE TWO

Carrying Rhythm into the Everyday

✣ In India, musicians may enter into what is called a *chilla,* a ritual retreat where they isolate themselves for as long as forty days and do nothing but play music. In this retreat of making sound and rhythm, the vibrations of your instrument take you inside new worlds of experience and awareness. Your instrument may come to life and teach you or you may become inseparable from the instrument you are playing.

When we fill ourselves with soulful rhythms and play them out in the world, we breathe soul into others. This is the case whether we're playing a drum, a musical instrument, speaking, working, playing, or being still. Soul is a condition of our presence, indicating whether we are in tune with the natural rhythms of life or out of step with them. When we bring soulful rhythms into breathing, work, play, discovery, invention, listening, speaking, and so forth, we bring soul into our presence and into the space where others reside.

You know when you have soul because it creates a stirring of energy within you. You feel that your inner music can pour forth onto the lives of others and that the tingling sensation of your heart can radiate a warmth into the world. This soul is not an understanding but a special way of being alive and present in the world. It is a passion for life that pulses itself through the consciousness of others. Whether it is labeled as charisma, love, energy, sexuality, magnetism, holiness, or spirituality, it is the rhythm of being alive that is recognized by all who are touched by it.

In 1665 the Dutch scientist Christian Huygens discovered that if you place two clocks next to each other, in a relatively short period of time they will start ticking in perfect synchrony. Called the Law of Entrainment, he found that two related rhythms that are close to one another will become entrained, that is, pulse to the same rhythm. It is a mystery as to why this takes place, but it occurs not only with mechanical clocks but with biological and sociological clocks as well. For instance, women in close groups often menstruate at the same time.

This is a fantastic notion to ponder when it comes to understanding our relationship to other rhythms in the world. Caught in universal, planetary, social, personal, and biological rhythms, we are unquestionably entrained to each other. Yet how aware are we of the ways we entrain one another with rhythms? Breathing soulful rhythms into everyday life involves entraining yourself and others with soul.

The Australian Aborigines don't have drums as we know them, but clapsticks to make rhythms for their songs and ceremonies. Following their example, obtain a pair of small sticks that you can strike together and produce a pulse at any time and place. Carry these with you, and when you feel that your situation requires some soul and vital life, pull out your sticks and strike them together. If you have to step away from a social group, then do so. If everyone is always dancing together, then the careful introduction of a new rhythm will pull the dancers into its beat. Introduce your pulse with good will for all. This pulse is a spiritual heart beat that will help open grace and compassion within others.

The deepest contemplative practices, whether they consciously specify it or not, bring about a momentary stillness that allow us to become re-entrained to the rhythms of life. Indigenous rituals sometimes involve entering mental states that are resonant with the earth's magnetic vibration. This frequency, known as the Schumann resonance, pulses at 7.8 cycles per second, the same beat as the lower alpha frequency of human brain waves, often associated with meditative states of consciousness. When we vibrate at this frequency we are literally tuning in to the vibration of the earth's soul. The Australian Aborigines have ceremonies where they spend the night singing sacred songs and thumping the earth with the intent of entering the vibratory realm of Dreaming. They purposefully attempt to vibrate at the same frequency as their original ancestors, the ones they believe dreamed the earth.

Seeing with Your Heart

♣ When our hearts are deeply touched, whether it's from seeing a new-born child for the first time or melting into the eyes of our lover, we see with our hearts. Passion washes away any meandering curiosity or critical inquiry and allows us to fully accept and unconditionally merge with the object of our attention. In this seeing there is less separation between the observer and the observed and the lover and the loved. We step outside of a judging eye and allow the beauty and holiness of the other to radiate a warmer and deeper seeing within our heart.

We may look at other children and not see their beauty as easily as we see it in our own offspring. This is simply because we don't look at them through our hearts. Heartful seeing is brought about when we resonate with the other and erase the difference between us. When we dance or play music in perfect rhythm with another person, we experience a connection that we don't forget.

As strange as it might seem, if two people who never have met before fall into a perfect dance with one another, where each step is in exquisite synchrony with that of the other, a small miracle takes place. Their relationship sacrifices each individual's separateness or I-it to become an offering to the altar of the I-Thou, where each person's performance fits with that of the other to make a complete whole. These magical moments of intertwined relationship may take place in all aspects of life, in art, sports, conversation, and laughter.

This experience of divine union is the core of mysticism and it is how the sacred light brings us into relationship with one another. It is a joy that is more blissful than any act of conventional sexuality and holier than any imaginable ceremony or ritual of devotion.

Whenever you catch yourself judging another person or yourself, you are not seeing through your heart. Try to find something about the other person that brings your heart back into your viewing. Perhaps you need to imagine them as they were as a child or as they will be as an elder. Can you see them with their own children or as a starving person desperately needing some food and water? What if they were disguised as an undercover angel, testing you to see whether you notice them? Imagine that they will someday save the life of someone you care deeply about, whether it's your child, friend, or significant other. No matter how disturbing they presently may be, see how differently you would observe them if you knew that they would significantly touch your relations in the future. Or as the Dalai Lama suggests, remember that we all are equal in that none of us wants to suffer and we're all seeking happiness. This remembrance helps bring the compassion we need to spiritually reach out to others. Do whatever is necessary in your imagination to bring your mind back within your heart so that you will feel the humanness and equality of other beings.

Seeing with your heart is an essential part of soulful living. It brings us into the deepest rhythms of everyday soul. It is not possible to bring forth deep matters of the soul unless you learn to see more heartfully. One of the most powerful guides to heartful seeing is to carry an awareness of the inevitability of everyone's death. You and everyone you meet will die someday and remembering this fact can be a strong wake-up call to feel differently about how we relate to one another. Given that our time on earth is precious and limited, how can we afford not to see through our hearts? Is there time to waste on heartless observation when our time with one another is so brief?

Open your heart to others so they may learn to see you through their heart. When two hearts see one another, each is given a spiritual blessing. This is the closest we get to seeing through the eyes of our Creator. As you learn to see this way, you will find yourself falling in love with the world.

EXERCISE FOUR

Opening the Hearts of Others

♪ When we see someone with our heart, they know it and begin seeing us that way too. Soulful spirituality celebrates the mission of opening the hearts of others. It works toward the enlightenment of everyone rather than the self-actualization of the isolated individual.

A graceful way of opening the hearts of others is to commit purposeful acts of celebration. Praise others for the tiniest acts of goodness that they bring into the world. Smile when they try to make positive contact with you and support every effort they make to deliver humor. Do not judge whether their performance deserves your praise but regard their effort as an invitation for you to help them bring more verve and vitality into their presence. Performers bring out their best when their audience brings it out of them. Consider everyone you meet as a performer who needs a great audience to bring out their best.

Being a member of the audience is also a performance, where we perform for the performer in a way that turns them into the audience. We are therefore both performers and audience members on the stage of life. Each is an act requiring total commitment to the performance in order to make us as alive and vibrant as we possibly can be.

Applaud every spiritual effort of others no matter how small you may think it is, and become a cheerleader for everyone's efforts to bring forth soul. Many of us do not know the secret that all professional en-

tertainers keep—that an audience may take you out of yourself and beyond your limitations, bringing forth a performance that stuns everyone. Similarly, we need to open ourselves to the passionate rhythmical
current that flows through a community of open hearts that seek to be
fully alive in the spirited performance of our life. We are all in this together, and anyone who is held back holds us all back. We must serve
bringing the light to everyone as the surest way of finding it ourselves.

The most enthusiastic human being I ever met was Heinz von
Foerster. One of the truly brilliant scientists of our time, he is a founder
of contemporary cybernetics. To be around Heinz is to experience
someone who is a prodigious listener. He hangs on every utterance you
offer, waiting to explode with enthusiastic support for ideas or fragments
of ideas that may lead you somewhere. Gleefully exclaiming, "Fantastic!" or "Wonderful!" Heinz fills you with feelings that your life is important and worth performing. I'm not speaking of a Pollyanna figure
but an extremely remarkable intellectual. He will challenge you when
you're off track, but he'll give a standing ovation to your genuine movements of being alive.

Consider that you do not really know other people unless you are
aware of the bliss they want to follow. Help them dream, find inspiration, and discover their bliss as a way of truly loving them. Nothing
brings forth more bliss than helping others find their bliss. When we
collaborate in the search for bliss, everyone is touched and fulfilled. The
road to a spiritual life is paved with many blissful moments, but none
more enlightening and inspiring and joyous than the bliss that takes us
across the abyss separating us from one another. There we find ourselves
inside the hearts of one another, dancing in the light of one spiritual
family.

❧

CHAPTER FIVE

The Dreaming:
Entering the Light of the Night

Oh, these humans of old knew how to dream and did not need to
fall asleep.

—FRIEDRICH NIETZSCHE

*I*N MY TRAVELS around the world I experienced a
wide variety of spiritual dreams. Sometimes the
dreams were lucid with ghostlike presences that gave me instructions
about a spiritual practice. At other times I would witness miraculous
visions, hear celestial music, encounter a divine luminosity, or feel my
body being touched by remarkable energies.

In the beginning of my spiritual odyssey I was more easily intoxicated by the "reality" and "power" of visionary experience and was
tempted to believe the seductive notion that they were evidence of extraordinary abilities that were available to me. This temptation of power
has touched the imagination of millions of readers through the literary
tales of well-known anthropologists and their accounts of a spiritual
lifestyle that seeks to accumulate personal power. This temptation,
however, can become a major roadblock on one's pathway to quenching the deepest spiritual thirst.

Spiritual elders from different traditions taught me that the thirst for spiritual knowledge and power is not that different from the unquenchable thirst of a psychological seeker. Turning life into a gigantic board game of hidden archetypal meanings and buried psychic treasures or an Olympic-like competition involving natural and supernatural "power moves" darkens the light that directs us to pure spirit. The experience of being psychic, of having precognitive dreams, and even of having healing powers are side effects of one's spiritual journey. They are not the core of what spirituality is all about. Getting attached to miracles and special powers is an example of getting trapped by what the Buddhist teacher Chögyam Trungpa called "spiritual materialism." The path of spirit always follows the heart, not the hunt for personal power or magical entertainment for the psyche. When dreams are used to feed the heart, they bring us closer to spirit. As our heart becomes more filled with spirit, we are less impressed and tempted by the flash of extraordinary power.

Extraordinary experiences can come through dreams. We must learn to respect the teachings of visionary experience but give them no inflated importance, seeing them as natural phenomena that simply come to you when you are open to receive them.

Margaret Mead once advised that it was good to have a religious experience, but also good to then get over it. In the same way, it is valuable to have spiritual dreams, but to get over the temptation to bestow any special honor on the dreamer.

One night while putting my eleven-year-old son to bed, I made a silent request that the world of spirit reveal itself to him. I was concerned that he and his friends were so deeply entrenched in toys, television, and designer sneakers and hoped that he would be shown something about spiritual reality.

Later that night I was awakened from my sleep by my son shouting, "Dad! Dad! Get in here!" I ran to his room to hear him say, "Something very strange just happened. I think it was a dream. I dreamed that I died and that I went to heaven. Then God came up to me and explained how everything works."

I was, needless to say, thrilled that my request had been granted. Much as I tried, I couldn't resist asking him what God looked like and what had been told to him. My son brushed me off with, "I'm too tired to talk anymore." And he went back to sleep.

The next day I asked if he remembered what had happened, and without a second to reflect he responded, "Yes, but don't be dumb!" We never have spoken about the dream. It has remained untouched by the limited abstraction of language but sits deeply in our hearts.

The holiest of dreams can seldom, if ever, be discussed. Gary Snyder once said that he never writes down his best poems. They typically take place when he is in the woods and they are too holy to be spoken outside of the moment and place where they were born. Spiritual elders advise us to never tell all of a sacred dream because its mystery and spirit may dissipate in the telling. And we may begin to get a swelled head.

Spiritual Dreaming

✣ In our time, dreams have been overromanticized, over-psychologized, and overinterpreted. We are drowning in what may be called "psychological dreaming," the mirroring and displaying of the fantasies, delusions, neuroses, desires, and fears of the ego-centered self. There we dream of being chased by bad guys, comforted by earthly pleasures, falling off cliffs, or flying to faraway places. When we are freed from our ego-centered self through compassion and getting into rhythm, it becomes possible to have a "spiritual dream," where we enter the imagination of a Mind that is greater than the one circumscribed by our self. Spiritual dreams, what some Tibetan teachers call "dreams of clarity," take place in a person whose ego-centered self has been quieted.

To better understand spiritual dreaming, I ask you to stop and think about the nature of the mind doing the dreaming. There are many ways of finding, seeing, falling into, and experiencing your mind. To begin with the most familiar form, there is the limited individual mind of the ego, which too often assumes that it is the only kind of mind in town. This assumption easily tempts us to believe that we are the sole possessors of intelligence and reason and therefore ought to be in charge of Mother Earth.

However, it is also possible to imagine nature as filled with other kinds of mental processes. When we link up with another human being it is possible to create a mind of relationship. This takes place when two lovers become one in their caress, or when dancers know exactly how their partner will perform, or when a basketball team effortlessly moves in synch with one another.

Not only is mind found in our relationship with other persons and processes, mind may be seen as imminent in the different systems and subsystems of our whole ecology. Gregory Bateson was an ecological visionary who regarded the largest imaginable mind as what people call God and saw it as the mind of the whole planetary ecology. Bateson's God is the Planetary Mind that dreams what the Australian Aborigines call the Dreamtime. Indigenous people have always known that nature has a mind that can dream and that if we open ourselves to being embraced by the greater mind of nature, then nature may dream us. This is the mind of the sacred. It is larger than the boundaries of our psyche and our social relationships. It is the mind of life itself, the web that creates and sustains our existence.

It is possible for us to enter these many minds. In all of these minds, the mind of individuality, the mind of relationship, and the mind of ecology, it is possible to dream. Spiritual dreams do not arise from an individual's psyche but from the broader minds of relationship and ecology. Indigenous traditions approach spiritual dreaming by stepping outside of themselves and acknowledging their relationships to family, community, and the whole ecology that holds their lives. Their thirst for spiritual direction does not drive them to acts of consumerism, where they go to market to buy themselves a vision, a psychic reading, or an entertaining dream. They self-lessly prepare to be touched and dreamed by a mind that can't be held, bought, or owned by any particular human being.

Blowing Your Mind and Falling into the Dreaming

♣ In the wake of a traumatic experience, you may be brought into the Dreamtime of spiritual dreaming. It almost always happens when you face death. Our limited individual minds aren't prepared to handle such an experience and all the inner fuses go out, leaving us open to having a visionary experience.

Your mind is like a circle that connects all of your ideas, emotions, and experiences. When the circle is opened, it becomes a partial arc that then may be linked within a larger circle. When we break open the closed circle of our individual mind, we literally become opened and available to enter into greater circles of mind.

However, if a psychiatrist or psychotherapist rushes in to help you through a shocking experience with medication and words of repair, any opportunity for spiritual development may be lost. What they do is patch the broken circle of your mind rather than encourage you to keep it open with the hope and trust that it will be embraced and linked within the larger mind. When the circle of our mind is broken, it becomes a thread, a line that may take us directly into the world of spirit and displays of sacred dreaming.

We have entered an age of open spirituality that permits us to enter the Dreamtime with less fear of social criticism. Even the world of sports is attuned to the athlete's attempt to fall into "the zone," the zenlike state of mind where optimal awareness and performance may be achieved. The idea of falling into alternative states of mind also applies to how we fall into the flow and rhythm of being in everyday life. The scholar of human experience Mihaly Csikszentmihalyi refers to this process as a "flow experience," where we become so involved in what we are doing that it no longer becomes a doing, but a way of being. The flow experience is a falling into a reality that does not separate the doing from the being. This is the reality of the dream.

In a way, all of our experience is dreamed, whether it be the dream of material reality or that of other realities. We are free to construct an infinitude of realities, where some are shared with others, while others are more private. The Harvard theologian Harvey Cox suggests that the next *Summa Theologica,* or major theological contribution, will recognize a multitude of different spiritual realities.

Protecting Mystery

♣ Sacred dreams need to be kept free of overinterpretation. When an explanation removes the mystery that a dream holds, then its spirit and soul have been slain. If an explanation has to be made, it should be directed by spirit and contribute to maintaining the mystery and soul within the dream.

Many people have difficulty living with mystery. The unknowable makes us uncomfortable and sets us off on a search to unlock its secret. The whole spectrum of spiritual experiences, from feeling energy blasts and seeing waking visions to near-death experiences, has brought forth the professional explainers to detail how we don't have to see them as mysteries but as readily explained brain waves, chemical

squirts, and levels of consciousness. Just because something is biologi-
cally induced, however, doesn't explain why it happens in the first
place. The origin of our experience remains a mystery.

When we hear reports of the world of clear spiritual dreaming,
whether they are from Aboriginal people or contemporary mystics, we
must be careful to note whether we are hearing it within the mind of
psychology or within a larger context. Indigenous traditions often pro-
hibit talking about spiritual matters and natural mysteries outside of a
spiritual context. I know medicine people who will never allow you to
tell them anything about spirituality unless they have first made a
prayer and given an offering of tobacco. This ritual brings the conversation, the telling and the hearing, into a sacred context.

Into the Dreamtime

❧ An elder Cheyenne medicine man, William Tall Bull, tells the story
of how one of his relatives was brought into the ways of spiritual medicine. After being on a hunt, he returned to camp and saw that his people had moved on. Rather than follow their trail he paid attention to
an old and sick blind dog that had been left behind. He decided to stay
with the dog so that he could feed it, care for it, and give it comfort
during its last days.

One night the man had a dream in which the dog came up to
him and spoke these words: "Thank you for opening your heart to me.
When you wake up, you will see that I am no longer alive. I want to
give you a gift as a way of expressing my appreciation for all that you
have done. Please take my eyelids and place them in a leather pouch.
People will come to you asking for help, particularly those who have
sickness in their eyes. Hold this medicine bag in front of them and you
will make them well." When the man awakened, he saw that the dog

had died. He took the eyelids and became known as a strong medicine man, particularly in the curing of snow blindness and eye problems.

The Dreamtime may also move right into the everyday when we are wide awake. Ikuko Osumi, Sen-sei, tells how a sacred white snake appeared to her when she was a small child visiting the shrine of her ancestor, Eizon Hoin, a famous seventeenth-century Buddhist priest. The snake came right up to her, told that he had supported and protected the family for many years, and that it was time for her to take over this responsibility. After that meeting, Eizon Hoin's spirit became her principal teacher and guide, always present when she conducts her healing work.

Vusumazulu Credo Mutwa describes his entry into the world of spirit as including multiple dream encounters with a tall black Zulu king wearing a black ring around his head who would always say to him, "You are named Vusumazulu, awakener of the Zulus, and you must help my people awaken." Over and over he would say this until Mutwa finally surrendered to his spiritual calling.

Among African-American Baptists, preachers were traditionally brought to their career through a powerful vision. Reverend Jefferson was such a Southern preacher who fasted in a graveyard while praying for a vision. He experienced God putting him on an operating table, opening him up, and giving him spheres of light. The experience healed the wounds of his life and gave him a new vigor and authority to preach and to heal others.

In North America, Ron Geyshick, an elder medicine man from the Lac La Croix reserve, described how visioned spirits now live inside his body. Within his right shoulder lives his strongest guide, an albino deer, while a regular deer lives inside his left shoulder. He has two moose spirits around his hips, just below the bone—a timber moose and a blue one. Jesus lives in his heart while four butterflies from around the world reside in each ear. He says that whenever their wings start fluttering, he sends his regular moose or the albino deer to find out what they're saying. Like other shamans and healers from other cultural traditions, this Ojibway medicine man lives with an entire ecology of spirits residing within his whole being.

In and Out of the Dreamtime

✣ Indigenous people throughout the world have understood how dreams may provide an opening or lifeline to spiritual realities. However, you don't have to be in the Australian outback to meet someone who has entered the Dreamtime. They come from everywhere, from a small rural community to a major urban city. My wife discovered that her colleague had entered the Dreamtime shortly after her father's death. The night after the funeral service she received a phone call from her father, who told her that he was all right and that he had not suffered in his death. She had been worried about him and the call gave her peace not only about her father but about her own life as well.

I have entered the Dreamtime in a variety of ways. One evening I woke up and saw a door in front of my bed that was partly opened. I went back to sleep and then woke up again, this time seeing the door completely open to the world of spirit. I have stepped into this other reality and have been shown the illness of someone else or been given specific information about spiritual practice. The Dreamtime is as palpable as any other reality, including the one in which you hold this book.

In the Gnostic Gospel of Thomas, Jesus discusses the sacrament of unity: "When you make the two one and when you make the inside like the outside and the outside like the inside, and the above like the below, and when you make the male and female one and the same . . . then you will enter [the kingdom]."

As we prepare our inner life for spirit, the natural world may be reborn within us through the greater Dreaming. In the Dreamtime we set forth on journeys that bring the outer into the inner. This boundary or crack or lifeline between the inner and outer world becomes deeper and wider with every crossing until one day the space in the crack has become the whole. This whole space that once separated the inner from the outer becomes the sacred emptiness that now embraces the entire universe.

Sometimes the crossings into the Dreamtime shatter all of our beliefs in the difference between the world of imagination and the world of the material. An Ojibway man told me he dreamed that his grandfather took him to a secret ceremony where the men sat around a circle wearing the masks of different animals. At the end of the ceremony his grandfather came to him and painted a red stripe on his hand. Startled by the realness of the dream, he woke his wife to tell her what had happened. At the end of his story, she pointed out that his hand actually had a red stripe on it.

In the Dreamtime, anything may take place, but don't be overly serious about your dreams. They should not be given any overimportance nor should we become pious about the revelations they seem to convey. An old shaman once remarked to his apprentice, "Last night we flew with the gods, but now we're idiots again. Back to the cornfield!" After we soar into the highest realms of the Dreaming, we must recognize that we have returned home again where we must rub our hands together and go into the new day eager to bring revitalized life and vision into our work.

The Transforming Midpoint

♣ The difference between the real and the unreal is an opposition which hides the greater truth that simultaneously sees both views. When you accept two contrary perspectives, you give birth to a new experience.

This process of integration is something like Sir Charles Wheatstone's invention of the stereoscope. In 1838, he made two drawings of a cube and held them in front of him. One drawing was of how the block looked when seen from the perspective of his left eye, while the other drawing was from the perspective of his right eye. He then set up some mirrors that enabled him to look back at the drawings at the same time, seeing simultaneously with his right eye the drawing made from the right-eye perspective and the left eye seeing the drawing from the left-eye perspective. What he saw was a convergence of the different two-dimensional drawings—what he beheld was a three-dimensional block. When we bring different views in front of us and find a way to see them simultaneously, we are lifted to a higher order of seeing. The midpoint between contraries is a place of great transformational power.

Dreamtime is the place where opposing truths converge into different ways of seeing, hearing, feeling, knowing, and participating in the world. In the Dreamtime we are lifted into a multidimensional view of life in which different and often contradictory understandings of life are converged and transformed.

EXERCISE ONE

Daydreaming about Night Dreaming

♣ What would be the most meaningful dream for you to receive? Daydream about this dream until you feel like you have a sense of it. Draw a picture of this vision, but let no one else see it. If you are not sure about what to draw, then hold a pen and scribble something while you realize what the dream would feel like. When the drawing is complete, go to a copy shop and make a reduced copy. Reduce it over and over until it is the size of a postage stamp.

Place this tiny image inside your pillow. Think about it before you go to sleep and appreciate opening yourself to new ways of entering into the world of dreams.

Spend more time daydreaming about the night dreams you can't remember. Think of your daydreams as the dreams you had the night before but could not recall. Consider a number of imaginative possibilities: What if you kept repeating the same night dreams and that having a new night dream required having a daydream that day? What if daydreams are the deeper dreams and night dreams are merely rehearsals for daydreaming? And finally, what if daydreaming is the reverse side of night dreaming, so that finding the night dreams you can't remember involves imagining the opposite of what you daydream?

Use your daydreams to come up with all kinds of imaginary ways that your daydreams can be related to your night dreams. Use this imaginative play to create daydreams about the spiritual dreams you hope will come to you in the night. As you bring night dreaming into your daydreaming and open new possibilities for your day dreaming to come into your night dreaming, you will build a stronger lifeline to spirit.

EXERCISE TWO

Catching a Dream

❧ The Ojibway Indians make what they call "dream catchers," sacred objects that look like circular spider webs within a twisted branch of a tree. These webs are believed to catch any harm that might be in the air in the same way that a spider's web catches and holds whatever it comes into contact with. When kept over your bed, it helps filter out the bad dreams while allowing the good ones to pass through.

Set a net underneath, or next to, the place where you sleep. Make the net out of string or thread, or buy one that is already made. Every night before going to sleep, touch this net and ask that it help you catch a dream. On a small piece of paper, the same size that you would find inside a fortune cookie, write down one word that best represents what you want the dream to bring. Perhaps this word is joy, or hope, love, direction, creativity, healing, light, wisdom, luck, energy, vision, spirit, soul, rhythm, opening, faith, heart, peace, blessings, or enlightenment. Place it in the net.

Over time you may want to try different ways of setting your net. Move it around to different places, try different colors, shapes, and textures of paper or other material. Perhaps you will attach a special stone, coin, or momento to the paper that makes it more visible and enticing to spirit.

This action sends a message through your body and whole being that you are committed to receiving a dream and that you are willing to patiently go through this ordeal in order to receive one. Like a good fisherman, you will wait however long it takes to bring in a catch. As you act out seeking your dream, imagine that the world of spirit will be looking at you, checking whether you are really sincere, mindful, and heartful about catching a dream. Do whatever is necessary to show your sincerity, whether it involves creating a formal request, singing or chanting, performing a dream dance, laying out offerings, or making symbolic gestures. Do these things only if they move you to fall into the kind of sincerity you believe will touch the heart of spirit.

Do not be afraid to ask for dreams that will help you spiritually develop. Mama Mona Ndzekali, the great healer from Soweto, South Africa, says that unless we ask for guidance, we can't expect it to come. Think carefully about what you feel you need for your own spiritual growth and then request it. And be cautious: You may get what you ask for.

When a dream comes, examine it carefully and decide whether you will keep it or throw it back into the spiritual water where it came from. We always have a choice over what to do with the spiritual offerings that are presented to us. We can choose to let them go if they don't feel right for us. Sometimes we are tested to see if we will wisely give it away. Among some Native American Indians, spirits are seen as occasionally playing with us and may tell us the opposite of what we should do in order to teach us to rely more upon ourselves rather than become overly dependent on messages from other realms. The question as to whether a dream is sacred and from your Creator was once put to an Indian master named Mother Meera. She answered, "If it makes you more humble, then it is from God. If it fills you up with self-importance, then it comes from somewhere else."

Dreams should be considered living things. When one comes into the world, consider it a new birth into your life. Welcome its arrival with a celebration even if it only involves saying, "thank you." You may want to show your gratitude by actually writing a letter of appreciation. Store the letter and wait several months before mailing it to yourself. This will honor your dream and help keep its memory alive. You may also want to bring home flowers every time you are blessed with a spiritual dream or treat your friends to a special feast or dessert. Everything you do to show your appreciation for a dream is a way of making it more likely to influence you. It also helps bring forth other dreams that are related to the one that came. The more you feed a dream, the more likely it will become bait that attracts other dreams.

Indigenous people set out an offering to the spirits that watch over them and for the spiritual visions that come. This may be a bowl of fruit with a cup of water or it may be something special that you make. Examine your dream and see if there is a way of making something that is related to what was presented in it. Was there a color that made the dream unique? If so, then bring that color into your everyday life. Was there an object that can be made or found? If words were uttered, then find a special way to paint, carve, or write some of these words down. The more you bring your dream into the world, the more it is fed and made into a rich and fertile influence.

EXERCISE THREE

Stimulating Your Unconscious with a Bedtime Story

Live with the following stories for a while. They are designed to stimulate your unconscious and to help your day and night dreaming become more actively related. Read one story before you go to bed each night. You have six stories, so it will take six nights to read them all. On the seventh night, give yourself a break from the story telling, but start the stories again the following night. Go through six weeks of this until each story has been slept with a total of six times.

When you have a dream, write it down and note what story was read before you had it. The next week when you read that story, also read the dream you had with it. If you have another dream that night, add it to the story for the following week. When you read the following bedtime stories, do so slowly and out loud if you can.

The First Cup

The first mystical cup was found beneath a blue stone in Ireland. The boy who found it never told anyone what he had discovered. Every night before he went to sleep he would take out his cup and hold it in front of him, staring into its empty space. It brought many mysterious dreams into his life, dreams about the world of spirit.

For every dream it gave the boy, a tiny white feather grew out of the cup. By the time the boy had become an old man, the cup had grown a pair of perfectly shaped wings. One night the old man heard a voice that asked him to jump inside the cup. This is how the man was swallowed by the cup and moved into the heavens above.

The next morning all that was left in his bed was a cup with one tiny white feather inside it. On its surface these words were engraved: "For each dream that you swallow, feed me a white feather. Over time you will discover the wings that bring you home to spirit."

From that day onward, people ceremoniously honored the winged cup. Not only did they dream it into their lives, they carried it with them wherever they went. Some were even blessed with white feathers that would now and then come their way.

Brothers of the Trees

In the deepest forest of Europe, a group of monks decided to take a vow of speech abstinence. Instead of speaking, they uttered sounds that expressed their devotion to God. At first they expressed choral-like tones with simple harmonic structures. Then there came a day when one of the monks received an ecstatic vision. To everyone's surprise he began chirping like a bird. His joy spread throughout the community and each of them began chirping like birds.

For the first time they believed they had learned how to make a pure prayer. To protect themselves from a public who might not understand, they retreated deeper into the forest. Building living quarters that resembled great nests, they lived in the trees. There they also constructed a magnificent tree-house chapel. All the birds in the forest became their teachers and taught them many songs.

God was pleased with these devotees to such an extent that the gift of illumination was bestowed upon the entire community. Each brother was given a pair of luminous wings that enabled him to lift his spirit into the heavens. There they sang the melodies of all the wonderful birds, pleasing the angels and celestial hosts. To this day their music can be heard when people are inspired and moved into the highest peaks of spiritual bliss.

Dancing in the Dark

A beautiful young woman came to the dance studio late one evening and without knowing why decided to move with absolutely no constraints. To her surprise, the lights went out and she was left dancing in the dark. A wind could be heard blowing underneath her feet, and for a moment she thought she was floating above the floor. To dance without sight was a thrill she had never known before. She entered the dance of dreamers and opened her heart to ecstasies beyond her wildest imagination.

Not a week passed by without this woman dancing in the dark. She brought others into the dark and together they learned how to move through the unseen. As her body was freed from sight, it began to move in ways that were unfamiliar to her. Her chest would ripple waves of energy and her palms would pulse with rhythm. There were even times when she could feel the legs of other dancers who were completely across the room. The boundaries of her skin evaporated into the edgelessness of the dark.

The energy of this dancing was so profound that people in neighboring buildings reported healings and miracles spontaneously taking place during the time the dance was going on. It didn't take long for the public to insist that the dance be performed in all the great concert halls of the world. Off she went to every city, dancing in completely dark theaters in auditoriums where nothing could be seen but where the audiences were moved to feel everything.

The End of Belief

An Aboriginal elder once dreamed about a middle-aged nurse and youth guidance counselor who had written popular books on spirituality and were presently conducting workshops in the most luxurious hotels in Sydney, Australia. In the Dream she approached them and said, "You know nothing. Follow me and I will teach you about the Greater Nothing."

The nurse and counselor were shaken by the presence of this holy woman and found it impossible to resist her invitation. Off they went into the Australian outback, wondering what mysteries would be revealed to them.

After several days of driving they ended up in an old cave with ancient magical drawings painted on the walls. On the ground before them was a gigantic stack of paper with a couple of writing pens. Another elder woman entered and smudged them with thick smoke, followed by a group of elders coming forth and singing a song that was filled with much laughter and joy. The woman who had picked them up never took her eyes off of them and they realized that their lives were now completely in her hands.

She nodded to the council of elders and a profound stillness overtook the cave. Quietly she told them that they must spend the night in the cave, writing down every single belief they have, one belief for each piece of paper. They must do this as if their life depended on it. She announced that she would return in the morning and tell them what to do next.

That evening the nurse and counselor wrote their beliefs on hundreds of pieces of paper. They did not leave out a single belief. The next morning the elder returned and, looking at the pile of work they had done, burst into a large smile. She told them to grab their beliefs and follow her. Back into the jeep they went and for two more days they traveled until they were just outside the border of Sydney where their trip had begun.

"Now listen carefully to what you must do," the elder began. "First choose yourself a direction. Listen for where your heart feels drawn. Then face that direction, place a piece of paper in front of you, and walk ten steps forward. Place another belief on the ground and walk another ten steps. Continue doing this until all the pages holding your beliefs have ended. At this point, lie on the ground and speak these words into Mother Earth, 'I have come to the end of my beliefs.' This is the exact place where you must begin learning how to listen. Do not leave that spot until you have heard the truth of silence."

The Sacred Hole

In the hills of South Dakota is a sacred hole in the ground that was made by the coyotes over a hundred years ago. On the night of a full moon, these four-leggeds would enter these spaces after singing an inspired song to the Great Spirit. Then they prayed throughout the night to be taken to the spirit world where they hoped to be made whole.

As the coyotes practiced this ceremonial burial, a medicine woman began hearing their prayers in her dreams. She heard their request for guidance and prayed along with them, asking how she as well as the coyotes could be made whole. In a vision she was shown how to wrap herself in a special robe and walk to a sacred site where she would find a hole dug in the ground. She followed her vision and went out to place herself into the earth on the night of a full moon.

There she heard the coyotes singing all around her while she prayed with all her heart to the Great Spirit. What she didn't know was that there actually was a coyote in another hole no more than twenty-five yards away. This coyote was also praying and hoping that spirit would bring it a blessing. The two of them spent the night together that way, praying to the same Creator who had arranged for them to be neighbors that night.

About an hour or so before sunrise, the woman began to sing a prayer that honored the love she had for her children. Hearing it, the coyote believed the Great Spirit had answered its prayers and had come with the blessing of heartfelt music. With joy, the coyote sang with more passion than it had ever expressed, which the woman heard and believed was the voice of her Creator answering her prayer. She wept with gratitude, realizing that the most sacred teachings can only be conveyed through the music of the heart.

When the sun first appeared, both the coyote and the woman came out of the earth. With utter astonishment they became aware of each other. They soon realized that the Great Spirit's true gift had been placing them next to one another so that each could bless the other. Since that time they regularly meet at their sacred site and surrender their hearts to sing and dance under the light of a full moon.

The Garden of Words

There was an English gentleman who wrote many fairy tales for children and adults alike. When he retired, a little fairy visited him in the middle of the night and gave him these special instructions: "Go through all you have ever written and choose the sentence that pleases you the most from every story. Purchase a packet of seeds for each sentence. Now use the seeds to write these sentences on the soil. Do this for every tale and wait for the garden that comes forth."

The retired author faithfully executed this task and planted over five hundred and fifty-five packets of seeds. He spread these seeds over the side of a gorgeous hill in the countryside and watered them each day with loving care and eager anticipation of their future revelation.

When the seeds burst forth into beautiful flowers, the world was amazed to see that they appeared as the face of a goddess. The whole side of the hill looked like the face of the most beautiful woman anyone had ever seen. Children begged their parents to take them to see this face and a pilgrimage began from every corner of the globe.

The flowers never died. They always remained in full blossom no matter what kind of weather fell upon them. The garden became the most cherished and adored wonder on earth.

❧ As you tell these stories, change them in any way—altering the characters, the setting, the details, the beginnings, middles, and ends. Use them as preliminary structures for making your own bedtime stories. Invite your daydreaming to create bedtime stories for your night-time dreaming. As more stories, fairy tales, and fantasies are brought into your life, your dreams will be drawn out as they recognize a familiar voice.

EXERCISE FOUR

Tying a Cord to Spirit

❧ Mystical traditions throughout the world propose that we each have an invisible cord that is attached to our belly button region and connected to our "dream body," an ethereal counterpart to our physical body. This spiritual umbilical cord enables us to move our consciousness into the world of pure imagination, the home for other worlds of spiritual experience. Rather than getting caught in any intellectual arguments concerning the validity of these claims, let me simply say that in the reality of dream we may find this cord and use it as a lifeline to spirit.

With this image in mind, set yourself on a mini-journey to find a photograph or poster that you believe captures what the spiritual world looks like. It doesn't matter if this is a portrait of a religious icon, a fantasy-like rendering, an abstract painting, or an Aborigine dot painting. What is important is that it deeply touches you. When you find this symbol, regard it as your "soul image" and attach it (or a copy of it) to your bedroom ceiling directly over where you sleep.

Now securely attach a piece of silver or white thread to the center of this image and allow it to hang over your bed. This thread is a pathway that runs beside your cord to the spiritual world. It will help you to be carried and dreamed into spirit.

There are many rituals for dreaming that can help bring us to spirit. I once worked with a Cree man who was distressed because he never had any visions. We made a circle underneath his bed with twelve tree branches arranged like a clock. When he placed tobacco in the center of this circle and then went to sleep, he couldn't stop having powerful dreams that included flying out of his body, visiting his past, and healing himself in the present.

If you want spiritual dreams to come forth, then you must sincerely call out for them through requests and rituals that enact your desire to be related to the Dreamtime. If you sincerely ask for spirit to teach you in this way, then it will happen. If you wake up not remembering what you were taught, then regard this as evidence that you dreamed at a level deeper than your conscious mind could hold or understand. Wait to see what you learned from your evening dreams, whether you remember them or not, by looking for the learning to show up during the day, whether it is a new feeling, a special kind of silence, the courage to act in a different way, or a deeper realization of faith.

As we enter the Dreamtime, not only may encounters with spiritual beings and realities take place, but encounters with sacred luminosity are possible. In the Dreamtime, we find an invitation to open our eyes in the dark so that we may see the light of the night.

Spiritual dreaming, the practice of the night, helps fill our everyday life with dreams that open the heart and make us soulful vessels for spirit. Learn to be more awake in your dreams and more dreamy in your everyday wakefulness. This dreaming will help awaken your spirit and bring you into visions of clarity, the sight of the greater Mind of nature. Celebrate the night as a time for learning how to enter the day and welcome the day as an occasion for breathing night-time soul into every ray of daylight.

3 ♣ Living with Mystery

CHAPTER SIX

❧

Awakening the Spirit: The Reception and Nurturance of Vital Life Force

Re-examine all you have been told at school or church or in any book, dismiss whatever insults your own soul, and your very flesh shall be a great poem and have the richest fluency not only in its words, but in the silent lines of its lips and face and between the lashes of your eyes and in every motion and joint of your body.

—WALT WHITMAN

I HAVE WITNESSED HEALINGS throughout the world, in ceremonies, church services, and in the private sessions of spiritual healers. They may involve a frenzy of activity that takes place in the Bushman healing dance or a more constrained gentle touch or wave of the hand in a solemn ceremony. In the rainforests of Paraguay, I watched the elder Guillermo Rojas, referred to as the "Holy Father," heal an adolescent girl who had abdominal pain. The entire community gathered in their ceremonial hut where the women sang songs while the men danced around a canoe that served as an altar. Finally, the girl was brought forward, and Guillermo took out a wand of feathers and began waving it over her body. He then dipped the wand into some milklike substance that was in the canoe and sprinkled her with it. The girl was freed of her pain and subsequently remained in good health.

Some of the greatest healers know what the illness is before the client utters a word. Ikuko Osumi, Sen-sei, does not need to interview her clients. She immediately knows not only their present symptom but their medical history. She gave me my medical history the first moment I met her. She knew nothing about me, spoke no English, and had never met my translator. She uses her hands in a variety of ways to bring about healing, from a gentle touch to a rigorous manipulation of the other person's body. I have met and watched her work with numerous clients, including a business executive who was diagnosed with untreatable liver disease at the Mayo Clinic. After working with Osumi, Sen-sei, he achieved freedom from his disease and a good state of overall health.

I have personally received the touch of healing from my wife, Marian, who touches me with her right hand and then becomes very still as she prays for healing. Her hand becomes very hot, sometimes so hot I think I might get burned, and then my pain goes away. I have also received healing from others where I felt nothing while they did their work, but afterwards my symptom had disappeared. Once after conducting a ceremony for nearly four hundred people in Santa Clara, California, my lower back became strained, making it difficult for me to stand or walk. One of my helpers gently touched my back, and although I did not feel any heat or tingling as she did this, the pain disappeared and I was able to walk with no difficulty.

The Aborigines of Australia, the Bushmen of Southern Africa, the ancient Hebrew prophets, Jesus and his disciples, Muhammad, the ancient Egyptians, and all indigenous traditions have healed through touching one another in a sacred way. Jesus went as far as to differentiate the true Christian in this manner: "These signs shall follow them that believe: In my name . . . they shall lay hands on the sick and they shall recover." More than 1,300 years before the twelve disciples were born, Akhenaton of Egypt was healing others in the same fashion. Like the Kalahari Bushmen and the Australian Aborigines before him, an energy was transmitted into the bodies of others to bring about healing.

The Aboriginal *wirinum,* or medicine person, tunes into spiritual energy like we tune in a radio station. The wirinum seeks a particular vibration and brings it into his body. This energy, which they call *turnpinyeri mooroop,* is plastic and movable and is the same as the *seiki* felt by the Japanese practitioner of seiki-jutsu and the *num* of the African Bushman and the Holy Spirit of the Christian. When it is shared through touch with the deepest desire to help another person, it brings about vitality and well-being.

This spiritual practice is as natural as breathing. Among the oldest indigenous people, it is considered the most vital aspect of day-to-day spirituality. I am referring to the practice of opening yourself to the direct reception and nurturance of spiritual energy. It is the fuel for creative expression, imagination, and health. All that we have said in this book so far has been about preparing ourselves to be open, available, and ready for contact with this energy.

When we fill ourselves with vibrant spiritual energy, it pushes out the tired states and feelings that have accumulated in our body. If we do not have a way of getting rid of the "tiredness" of each day, we make ourselves vulnerable to illness. Traditional healers aim to move spiritual energy through others as a way of helping them maintain health, whether this process is conceptualized as the movement of chi in acupuncture, the transmission of *seiki* in the Japanese practice of seikijutsu, the circulation of kundalini in yoga, the boiling of *num* among the African Bushmen, or the baptism of the Holy Spirit in Christian services. Some of the oldest traditions of healing refer to this energy as

medicine, and shamans, healers, and medicine people give their lives
to helping others receive it.

Num *and the Kalahari Bushmen*

The Kalahari Bushmen belong to one of the oldest cultures on earth.
They are regarded by other African healers and spiritual leaders as the
holders of the strongest medicine on their continent. I believe that they
practice one of the purest forms of healing and have much to teach us
about the transmission of spiritual energy.

They call this energy *num* and believe that it can be aroused,
heated, and moved in your body. The stomping of feet in a healing
dance helps stir up the *num*. It is similar to the vibrating energy we feel
before we go on stage or in front of an audience. Having butterflies is
a perfect expression for describing the initial stirring of this spiritual energy. You feel both excited and nervous at the same time.

Imagine amplifying this internal fluttering until you are so excited
that you begin to fear losing your balance and stability. If unchecked,
you realize that you will lose control of yourself, and if it continues even
further, you will truly lose yourself. We typically find a way to calm
down our butterflies rather than let them get to this point. Among the
Bushmen, however, the internal energy is encouraged to heat up.

When you have a bellyful of boiling energy, you decide either to
allow it to dissolve your sense of self and psychological identity or you
cool it down and return to the sobriety of normality. If you sacrifice
your self, you will be carried outside the boundaries of your individualized mind and have a kind of psychological death experience. You
cross over into a fully awakened spiritual state of being where energy
naturally moves through your body, particularly through your hands.
The energy subsequently may be transmitted into other people by
touching them, and a wide array of spiritual experiences may take place

and bring forth what is probably the most powerful healing experience of our lives.

I traveled to the central Kalahari Desert in Africa and experienced the Bushmen's way of healing. They gave me a home under a camelthorn tree and with an open heart I received the oldest form of healing in the world—the touch of an energized body. Throughout the globe I have met healers who move and touch in this way, bringing spiritual energy into the bodies of others.

Seiki

Ikuko Osumi, Sen-sei, is one of the last living masters of a healing tradition called seiki-jutsu that involves the direct transmission of *seiki*, the old Japanese word for vital life force. She invited me to live with her so she and her assistant, Takafumi Okagima, the only other living Japanese master of this practice, could "fill me with *seiki*."

She told me that the first time she gave *seiki*, her teeth fell out. It had taken her many years to master this ancient healing practice. She said that *seiki* comes to her from the atmosphere and concentrates into a whirlwind that enters her ceremonial room. Some of her clients report seeing these whirlwind-like clouds enter the room when she transmits *seiki*.

My week of preparation was marked by perfect fall weather with the sun shining every day. On the evening before the ceremony a thunderstorm broke out and the next morning the wind was blowing harder and harder until every door and window in her house rattled and shook. As typhoon conditions came upon Tokyo, she and her assistant said they couldn't hold the *seiki* any longer and that it was time to transmit it.

I entered a small room and was carefully positioned on her *seiki* bench. The next thing I remember was hearing strange noises, feeling the wind blowing, and being aware of a ring of heat and electrical energy on the top of my head. My body jolted and I felt like I was wired directly to an electrical spiritual current. After I received this current, I felt a deep sense of peace and calm. For months after, I felt deeply in rhythm with life.

After this ceremony I was taken to another room to rest and there I reflected on the familiarity of this experience. It was the same transmission of energy I had felt in the African-American church, in the South American rainforest among the Guaraní Indians, in ceremonies of Native North American Indians, in the Kalahari with the Bushmen, and elsewhere. Everywhere in the world this energy exists and is used for healing and awakening spiritual experience.

Awakening the Spirit

♪ Mama Mona Ndzekali, a deeply respected healer from Soweto, turns on jazz music and falls into its soulful rhythms when she prepares to bring forth this energy in a healing. Music is a powerful tool to ready the body for receiving spiritual energy. Aldous Huxley remarked that it would be impossible to listen to the drums of an African ceremony and not have a spiritual experience.

When soulful rhythms enter, they cause your body to move and pulse with the beat of the music. If you don't hold back, this rhythm can turn your body into a musical instrument. Like the pulsing skin of a drum or the vibrating string of a piano, you move, and in this movement your body carries the spiritual energy. Your movement may be wild and frenzied or it may be an internal vibration that is invisible to an outside observer.

I asked Osumi, Sen-sei, to watch a film of a Bushman healing ceremony. After viewing it she told me that they heal in the same way as her tradition of seiki-jutsu. Spirit awakens when a healer disseminates vital life force into another with vibrating hands and movements of a shaking body filled with heat.

Many people who have received this energy have described it as an intensification of all the senses. Each encounter with the energy is unique for the person receiving it. Some people report a floating sensation and a desire to spontaneously move their body. Sometimes the person receiving the energy begins shaking, and over time they may even begin transmitting it to others.

While one is passing on this energy, there is no sense of self or of being the one who is doing the passing. As Black Elk described it, "Of course it was not I who cured. It was the power from the outer world, and the visions and ceremonies had only made me like a hole through which the power would come to the two-leggeds. If I thought I was doing it myself, the hole would close up and no power would come through it." Similarly, William Blake acknowledged that "I myself do nothing. The Holy Spirit accomplishes all through me." The person who is regarded as giving the transmission is actually no more than a midwife who simply helps to make its delivery.

In ancient healing practices, such as those conducted by the African Bushmen, this energy work almost always takes place in community. If anyone gets filled with energy, even if it's during the course of everyday activities, they immediately pass it on to each other. It is not kept inside but freely exchanged. In this same spirit, do this work with a spouse, companion, partner, or friend. If you have no one else to work with, then do it with a pet dog or cat. Gently place your hands on them and vibrate the energy into their whole being. You can even go into the countryside or your own backyard and place your hands and feet into the soil, so that the energy may circulate into the earth. Never hold the energy inside, but share it with other living beings.

The most common advice given by spiritual elders to their apprentices who are beginning to work with spiritual energy is to "push the plate back when your belly is full." If you continue eating after you are full, you shouldn't be surprised if you subsequently become sick. The same holds for spiritual work. Never take in more than you can digest. One of the most common mistakes among well-intentioned spiritual seekers is the desire to move too fast. People too often want to learn everything overnight. You must proceed one bite at a time, allowing each moment and experience to be fully digested into your whole being. This is the most fulfilling and successful way to move forward on your spiritual journey.

How do you get this energy? Once you've been touched by a powerful current of it, whether it is from another healer or from the heavens, it is always with you and available to use with others. Many healers were literally hit by spiritual lightning or by a strong rush of energy that initiated them into this practice. You don't have to be struck by lightning to get the energy going. Anything that arouses your body to enter an excited energetic state can be used to jump-start the flow of this current. Listening to soulful music, remembering a powerful spiritual feeling, or praying for spirit to move you are several of the ways others use to get the energy moving.

Pay more attention to the kinds of activities that you feel increase enthusiasm. Perhaps it's a live musical performance, disco dancing, going wild at a sports event, singing at the top of your lungs in the shower, or simply hanging around a high-energy public place. Free yourself to enter more fully into these scenes and allow their energy to ripple through you. Allow a muscle to twitch or a limb to move when you feel the vibrations meet your body. When you first feel touched by a ripple of excitement, realize that energy is now entering. Move your body so that the energy may more freely circulate.

If you open yourself to spiritual energy and do so with a desire to freely share it with others, then you should proceed to do so with no fear or hesitation. There are many ways to initiate your introduction to this energy, including seeking out a practitioner or teacher of an energy-based healing art, such as reiki, jikyo jutsu, t'ai chi, seiki-jutsu, or the Chinese energy medicine called *qi gong,* which was documented in Bill Moyers's television series on healing. From within our own culture you can receive a "laying on of hands" from either a religious healing service or from a practice called "therapeutic touch," a form of energy work usually taught and administered by nurses. When you do this work, you will recognize the energy as a subtle warmth or tingling vibration in your body. With practice, you can learn to be more aware of it, move it around your body, and transmit it into others. Simply being near highly charged people and sacred places will help bring about a transmission.

Ecstatic Displays

✤ Powerful rhythmic drumming often precedes indigenous healing ceremonies. It brings soulful rhythms into the body of the healer and to all who open themselves to be touched by its energy. The sensuality of healing and spirituality is sometimes masked by contemporary religious institutions, perhaps because they fear that the wild energy might get out of control and turn into socially embarrassing forms of ecstatic display.

Many churches may not have recovered from the memories of the old revivalistic movements of Christian evangelism, particularly during the Kentucky Revival of the 1800s, when preachers would get their congregations so worked up that they would shout, cry, laugh, and even bark like dogs. At other times they might jump about for hours, hop around like frogs, or double themselves up while rolling on the ground like a hoop—the origin of the term "holy rollers." Another interesting ecstatic display was referred to as "the jerks," which one observer described as so frenzied that "they kicked up the earth as a horse stamping flies." During this time practically no one in a revival service was safe from being influenced in these ecstatic ways. Presbyterians, Methodists, Quakers, Baptists, and members of the Church of England were all touched.

The only people who were not ecstatically touched were those who went to the services with the primary intention to study them. As a turn-of-the-century reporter writes, "Those naturalists who wish to get it to philosophize upon it . . . are excepted from the jerks." Being energetically touched required avoiding the observer's position and going straight to the heart of the experience without an analytical mindset.

I have found that the form of expression that is displayed when people are highly charged with spiritual energy is largely influenced by the physical movements that are initially sanctioned. If a group sees someone laughing and it is socially approved by the people hosting and orchestrating the event, then others will fall into the officially sanctified expression of hysterical laughing. Whether it's an aesthetically pleasing form or not is determined by the choreographers of the spiritual ceremony, who, for example, in a Christian revival service would most likely be the minister, the deacons, and members of the choir.

Any form of body expression is possible, and as you move from one culture to another, the dance changes. The choreography for being spiritually energized is different among the African Zulus than it is for the Paraguayan Guaraní and the Native American Ojibway and Lakota. Some cultures are more structured about this expression, while others are almost completely improvisational and allow individuals to play it out in their own way. Dancing in this energy includes those who went to Beatles and Grateful Dead concerts and allowed themselves to scream, weep, and be completely swept away by waves of ecstatic delight.

I was taken to the mountains of northern Argentina by Armando M. Pérez De Nucci, an Argentine senator, physician, and faculty member of the Tucumán Medical School. Over the years he had worked with many of the traditional healers in the mountains outside of Tucumán and had written several books about them. Panta Leon Rios, a revered healer, told me how he began his work. When he was a young man he looked into a plate and saw the Holy Mother while the room filled with smoke. He had no idea what had happened to him but soon found that he had the ability to heal animals, particularly horses. He later began healing people through touching them and sending them energy through his eyes. He heals in a quiet way and says few words, but he exudes a deep sense of calm. The outside walls of his house are painted with scenes of children playing. His way of healing is gentle and the feel of his touch sends a soft charge of warm energy into your body.

When I first entered the home of Mama Mona Ndzekali, she paused to utter a prayer. Two professors from the University of South Africa accompanied me on my visit and they believed that she was the most calm and peaceful person they had ever met. In their words, "She must be a saint or an angel." She was very ill at the time and she said she wanted to pass on her spirit guides to me. I wasn't sure what she was talking about, but I allowed her to touch me, and as she did so I felt a current of energy move through my body as it shook from her transmission. She looked into my eyes and said, "I have seen the spirit of Jesus working through you. You must go to the church and pray your heart out."

I went to her local church in Soweto and prayed for guidance. I fell asleep and began dreaming of different faces including that of a nun. When I woke up I immediately left the sanctuary and without thinking walked around the entire church building and picked up three small stones. Later I described to Mama Mona what was etched on them—on one was a black cross, on another a circle with a barrel inside it, and the third stone had the head of a rooster etched on its surface. She let out a scream and said these were her lost healing stones and that years ago her spirit guides had told her that the stones would return to help someone else.

Mama Mona told me that her great-grandfather was Chief Mhlonhlo of the Mpondomise tribe, who was legendary for his spiritual powers. During the time when the Cape Town area was being settled, several unsuccessful attempts were made to capture him. Once his enemies approached his camp, and when they began to fire their guns a thick fog fell upon them, causing them to shoot each other in their confusion. Mama Mona received guidance and teaching from this ancestor as well as from her most powerful spirit guide, Sister Elize, a former Mother Superior.

I discovered that simply thinking about these spiritual images was an effective way of activating spiritual energy in my own body. I don't understand how this is the case other than it obviously brings back the memories of the powerful experiences I had with Mama Mona. She made it very clear that the source of all healing power is God, and that the power of prayer can result in a healing that takes place in an instant. Her healing work was usually accompanied by music, and the patients who received her touch often reacted as if they had received an electrical shock.

I don't know how to explain my experiences of her spirit guides or of those I have witnessed from my relationships with other spiritual teachers and healers. I believe that it is Osumi Sen-sei's love more than anything else that heals her patients. Her maternal presence brings forth a compassion and love that all of us long for even when we forget that we are looking for it. The same can be said for the gentle spirit of Mama Mona, a mother whose love not only touched her African community but thousands of lives all over the world.

The energy expressed by a healer is the same love that a mother and father have for their child. When you feel this love, it makes your body tingle as a child does when a parent showers them with the gifts of their hearts.

Wherever powerful energy is present, there is usually movement of bodies in a dance. The Gnostic Gospels tell us that Jesus taught his disciples how to perform a circular dance that brought about visionary experience. As they formed a circle and held one another's hands, Jesus began a chant that included these words: "To the Universe belongs the dancer. He who does not dance does not know what happens." The dance would enable them to experience his "mysteries."

Approximately one century ago a report was sent to the United States War Department that echoes what the Gnostic Gospels tells about "the dance of Christ." The document stated that Jesus was believed to be at Walkers Lake, Esmeralda County, Nevada, where Indians and white people were seen dancing together. The government report went on to claim that Jesus had gathered a large number of Indians and taught them a circular dance. He sang while they danced, and as he sang, he shook and trembled all over. Before he left he said that if they were good to one another, healers would be sent who could heal by mere touch.

This dance became known as the "Ghost Dance," and it is remarkably similar to the dance of Jesus in the Gnostic Gospels. It is also related to the healing dance of the Kalahari Bushmen and to that of many other spiritual ceremonies, including the dancing of the early Shakers, the Dance of St. John, which spread throughout Europe in the fourteenth century, the Deerskin and Jumping Dances of the California Yurok, and all cultural traditions from the Sufi to the Aboriginal that have used a sacred circular dance to inspire divine communion.

Dance moves people to give themselves to a rhythm that pulses and sometimes shakes their whole body. When fluttering hands pass this energy into another person, a healing interaction takes place, bringing us into the mind of relationship. There soul is expressed and our hearts are awakened to a deep realization of the truths and mysteries of spirit.

Healing Love

❧ Love untainted by fear, control, judgment, possession, and expectation is raw, vibratory life energy, the energy that can fill another person with the vital force of soul. It transcends ideologies, understanding, and social structures and is available everywhere. It is not bought, earned, deserved, or achieved, but is free to anyone who is sincerely open and empty. It may be found in the music of a jazz saxophonist playing in a sleazy bar as easily as it may be absent from a routinized ritual performed in an immense cathedral.

In the Kimberly area of Australia I visited a community of Aboriginal people. There I met Betty Johnston, a joyful woman in her late seventies who greets you with a big hug. Her hands move freely over your body as a way of getting to know you. Betty is a traditional healer who heals through touch. Like most revered healers she does not offer elaborate explanations of how healing works. "My healing comes from the heart where I just feel things," is the best way she describes her gift. People go to her and she hugs them and touches them all over, sometimes blowing air into their mouths or even giving them a little kiss. At other times she may "cry them back" by hugging them and crying together until the "sickness is cried right out of them."

Before I met Betty she had received a mysterious scar on her abdomen that looked like a spear mark. She explained that there are several emu next to her home that dream for her and that one of them had been speared, resulting in the scar on Betty's own body. Her mind and body are inextricably linked with the natural setting that holds her life, including its fauna and flora. In discussing these things, she does not hesitate to assert that the most important ingredient for bringing forth soulful spirituality and healing energy is belief. She tells us, "If you don't believe, nothin' gonna happen."

Faith is not an understanding that prepares us to take the leap. It is the leap itself, the plunge into the soulful rhythms and energies that promise to awaken our spirit and bring new life into our everyday. A life that is absent of the touch of spiritual energy is like life without breath.

EXERCISE ONE

Milking the Source: The Rocking Exercise

♣ One of the oldest ways of bringing spiritual energy into your body is to sit on a bench or chair and gently rock yourself, imagining that the motion you make is a milking of life's vital energy. Visualize your whole body drinking this spiritual water, soaking it up through every pore.

When you first sit down to do this practice, become as internally quiet as you possibly can. Then gently rock your body either forward and backward or to the sides. Do this purposefully in the beginning and wait for your body to fall into a natural rhythm that moves you to do it automatically. It will eventually feel like an external force is moving you without any effort on your part.

When the spontaneous rocking occurs, allow it to take you to deeper and stiller regions within your internal place of quiet. If you desire, make internal rhythmic sounds to accompany your movements and use them to take you more into your rocking. This practice can be done for ten to thirty minutes a day and is the most natural way you can nurture your internal energy.

After the rocking starts to take place automatically, you can begin future sessions in a different way. Lightly press your fingertips against your closed eyelids. This helps stimulate your nervous system to start the rocking motion. However, from time to time you may still want to jump-start yourself by imitating the motion at first while waiting for your body to naturally fall into it.

As you become comfortable with this practice, allow your hands to move over your body. They may gently touch, rub, vibrate, knead, or push various areas. Encourage your hands to have a mind of their own and liberate them to engage in any motion and action. If you feel stress or pain in a certain part of your body, let your hands decide where they will do their work. Sometimes they may go to another part of your body as an effective way of attending to the disturbed area. This practice not only helps you get rid of the accumulated toxins of each day, it brings you new energy. It is also a form for learning how to heal yourself. It is where your body and hands learn to move within the rhythms that are healing.

As you continue this practice you will awaken your innate ability to work with this energy in a healing way. Osumi, Sen-sei, uses this practice as a lifeline to spirit and as a direct avenue to many of its mysteries. If she has a question about her life, she will go to her *seiki* stool and place the question in her mind and then move into the rocking practice. In the stillness that the motion brings, a clue or answer is born.

Over time, your body will begin to do more than rock. It may make a wide variety of small and large movements. Some of them may even be classic exercises from other spiritual traditions that you have no conscious awareness of knowing. What makes this practice unique is that it follows the calling of your own body. The rhythms and motion of your body not only take you to where you need to go but also open up what you need to know.

If you like, follow the custom of seiki-jutsu and get a special chair or bench that is used only for this practice. You may use any seating arrangement that is comfortable for you as long as it enables you to easily maintain a natural rocking motion.

This simple practice brings to you the most perfect teacher you could ever find. This teacher is your own body. Learn to hear its call and move with it when it invites you to be in rhythm with its soul. The way in is through sitting down and finding that everything that you need has been waiting for you since the moment you were born.

EXERCISE TWO

Improvisational Touch

⚑ The other teacher that can help you is a relationship with someone with whom you have a deep commitment and trust. Begin this practice by sitting in front of each other and gently allowing your fingertips to touch. Encourage your fingers, hands, arms, and body to move as they feel called to do so. With time, the natural rocking and vibratory movements will come through both of you in a coordinated way. Quiet your mind so that your hands and body can learn to develop an inner radar that directs you to touch the exact spot the other person's body is asking to be touched.

Do this practice twice a week, but no more than every other day to allow enough time for the energy to digest. In the beginning, you may want to limit this work to thirty minutes, but with practice you will find yourself able to benefit from longer sessions. Approach this work in a ceremonial way, viewing it as a sacred occasion.

Your touch with one another should always be improvisational, that is, done naturally, and spontaneously without any conscious thought as to what you should be doing. Do not think to yourself, "I'll begin with the neck and then work myself down to the feet" like a massage therapist. Distract your mind with music, images, poetry, or whatever touches your heart and inspires you, without paying much conscious attention to the movement of your hands.

I was in an airport in Seattle when an old man came up to me and introduced himself as a teacher of Chinese medicine on his way to central China. He told me that he was frustrated with the American doctors he had tried to teach because they were more interested in memorizing the acupuncture points rather than learning to hear the patient's body calling them to a specific spot. Osumi, Sen-sei, sees our energy pathways as changing from day to day so that memorizing a fixed map of their whereabouts won't necessarily be useful in finding your way to where the patient needs to be touched.

Improvisation teaches us to be fully present and attentive to our immediate circumstances. Listen to how you can join with the ongoing rhythms of the other person. Move in a way that encourages the other to desire a collaborative relationship with you. In this way you are more able to join together in making some soul.

The art of improvisation utilizes whatever is given to you. Approach another person with no expectation of what they should have brought, but focus your attention to seeing what has been brought for you to play with. If the other person brings silence, then dance with it. If they are in another rhythm, move in synch with it. But never forget to introduce some surprise into your interaction, whether it be a sound, sight, touch, or movement. This is the syncopation that gives birth to the rhythms of soul. Without it you will be simply going through the motions. With it you awaken each other's spirit.

A large portion of soulful spirituality is about healing one another with touch. What you need to begin this practice is an authentic desire to help others and a willingness to simply touch them in a sacred way. In our efforts to awaken others to spirit, we help create an environment that facilitates our own awakening.

It is a good idea to say a simple prayer or blessing before you work with someone, such as, "I hope you will receive much happiness, joy, and blessings from this energy." When Osumi, Sen-sei, gave *seiki* to my eleven-year-old son, who is totally devoted to baseball, her blessing of prayer was, "This seiki will help make you a wonderful baseball player." Bless the other person by joining with their bliss and bring the energy into them with that bliss in mind.

You may also send energy to those who request or need healing, but are far away from you. Send the energy through your hands into the air and visualize a whirling wind taking it to them, entering the top of their head and slowly permeating through every cell of their body. Prayer and healing bring us closer to one another and help open our hearts to receive as well as transmit the gifts of spirit.

My dentist told me a story about a miraculous healing that took place in the high school near where I live. The star quarterback was making the final play of a football game when he was hit by a tackle who broke his arm. He was rushed to the emergency room, where the X rays revealed a major break in his bone. After the game, the entire team and coach came to see him and someone spontaneously led the group to pray that his arm be healed. The next morning the boy woke up and felt that his arm was no longer broken. He insisted that another X ray be taken, and to everyone's amazement it revealed a perfectly healthy and intact bone.

These stories exist in every community throughout the world. Remarkable recoveries and spontaneous cures help us to see that mystery is always present.

For those of you who have a loved one who is critically ill, it is natural to hope for a miraculous cure and it is natural to be angry with the entire cosmos for the pain you and your family are feeling. Be aware of the fact that it may be healing for you to express your rage toward the heavens. The Psalms teach us that articulating your rage against God can be a healing part of your prayer life. After you have purged your anger, despair, and frustration, begin asking for a spiritual resolution. Know that it is the energy of love that you are ultimately requesting. Healing does not necessarily mean that a medical cure will take place. It is about curing our hearts and making us more able to realize the soul of life, which sometimes includes its rhythmic breath between life and death.

Become a healing presence to others, touching them with your open heart and, when appropriate, your sacred touch. As you work toward awakening the natural ways within you that are capable of mobilizing the well-being of others, you will find yourself being healed. Heal others as a way of healing yourself.

EXERCISE THREE

Dancing in the Dark

❧ One of my favorite assignments for groups is to have them invent what they believe are new ways of dancing. We practice them for a while and then hold a special performance for the innovative dances to take place. One group sat underneath a table and only danced with their fingers, while another group invented a way of shadow dancing. Moving into the unimaginable frees us from worrying about whether we are dancing in the right way. Dancing in the dark takes the eyes of evaluation off us and we are more able to dance in the natural and unnatural ways that our body calls us to perform.

In an earlier chapter you were invited to meditate through creating internal rhythms that fit between the pulse of your own breathing.

Later you were asked to add internal music to that beat, and now I invite you to meditate not only with music and rhythm but with an internal dance. Visualize yourself and/or others dancing and allow your body to naturally rock with its motion.

Create a dance that is your personal signature in movement. Make up your own steps and add some unique moves to another form, or invent a completely different way of conceptualizing dance. Keep this dance a secret and only do it in private.

Use this dance when you feel stuck and need more movement in your life, whether it applies to your job, relationship, spiritual development, or game of golf. If you need a new insight regarding how to make a business presentation, go off and think about it while doing your dance. See it as a physical way of bringing some soul into the situation. Similarly, if you can't figure out what to say to your partner that will help your relationship move forward, then go to the dance floor. Any aspect of your life, from the practical necessities to the purest flights of fantasy, can be given to your dance.

We are in the habit of believing that our mind resides within our head. This understanding makes us too top-heavy. What we need is the more holistic realization that our whole body holds our mind. Whenever you now do some dancing, see it as your whole mind working.

When you dance, create rhythm, and make music; do not judge or evaluate your performance. Regard each of your performances as perfect and masterful. There is a method of psychotherapy in Japan that instructs the client to pretend that he or she is well. When you pretend that you are well, you develop an image of wellness and it helps you move toward health. In the expressive arts it is also beneficial to practice the posture of mastery. Remember that mastery has less to do with acquired expertise but is more a state of reception that captures artistic conception.

Go into your dance, your music, and your rhythms with the unwavering belief that everything in your performance is right on. The jazz pianist Oscar Peterson claims that there is no such thing as a "wrong note" to the pure improvisationalist. There are only particular outcomes that are to be improvisationally woven into the fabric of the ongoing performance. Each particular note, beat, and step has no meaning in and of itself but is given meaning by the way you bring it into the ongoing stream. If you accidentally hit a dissonant note, don't panic at the thought that you made a mistake. Celebrate the accident for its bringing in more surprise and syncopation—the heart of what we now recognize as soul.

EXERCISE FOUR

The Sacred Circle of Healing

❧ Through spirit the entire universe is available to you. You do not have to travel around the world in order to participate and benefit from other spiritual traditions. Spirit will bring whatever energy is necessary for you to receive.

With this in mind, sit down with a map of the world and use your imagination to fantasize about the diverse spiritual energies and offerings that come from different cultures and continents. Do not be concerned with accuracy but encourage your own voice to express its metaphors, feelings, beliefs, and free associations about the spiritual practices and resources that are available from different parts of the globe, particularly the ways they evoke spiritual energy.

Does the African continent bring forth a fantasy about raw, naked, spiritual energy that fills and moves bodies to dance wildly to the frenzied rhythms of ecstatic drumming? Do you see the Asian continent filled with disciplined practices of moving and transforming this energy? Are there visionary transformations taking place in your view of the South American rainforest and shamanic voyages into mysterious worlds being initiated around the Siberian Arctic? Are the hypnotic sounds of a didgeridoo being heard in Australia, and are whirling dancers moving through your mind as you scan the Middle East? Perhaps the desert regions of the world bring the sight of vision fasts and pilgrimages, whereas the majestic mountains invite you to hear the gods speaking directly to those who listen carefully on top of their peaks. Do the oceans, lakes, and streams provide baptismal waters for cleansing, and do the world's magnificent cities harbor hidden boxes of spiritual secrets, maps, and treasures to accompany you on your journey?

Create any image whatsoever in this global contemplation. Reflect upon what comes forth as a way of encountering your own relationship to the spiritual practices of other cultures. Create a circle as an image of the sacred circle that connects all traditions. It may be a zen-like stroke that exudes strength through its raw simplicity, or you may be inspired to create a collage of global spiritual images that are circularly linked.

Draw upon the images from your global contemplation and consider using them in your sacred circle or mandala. Do not stop with the making of one sacred circle. Keep creating new ones as your spiritual journey moves forward, and date each one so you can, over time, begin noticing how your spirituality changes and grows. See your image as always developing in the same way that Paul Gardner talked about art: "A painting is never finished—it simply stops in interesting places."

Find a special place to keep your artistic renderings. You may want to place a sacred circle over the area where you sleep and observe it prior to going to bed each night. Perhaps you will take it to a painter, sculptor, or carver, who would be commissioned to make it into a piece of art for your home.

Practice an awareness of your sacred circle to such an extent that it becomes as familiar to you as your own name. The rock star formerly known as Prince has already given himself a new symbol, and there is no reason why you can't also add the image of a sacred circle to your identity. A consequence of re-identifying yourself in this way is that you will be continuously reminded of your home in the center of diverse sacred traditions. In this way, you will begin feeling more and more related to the diverse spiritual energies of the world.

As you move toward accepting your sacred circle as an expression of your spiritual identity, begin using it when you meditate, pray, or sit in quiet contemplation. Shift your thoughts to the various parts of the circle, addressing each aspect or image with specific words or silence. With this practice, your meditating, praying, and healing will become circular rather than locked in one direction. It will also become more embedded within an ecology of global spirituality.

With this circular movement inside a spiritual ecology, you will become more open to diverse spiritual energies. The expression and quality of these energies will change as you draw them from different cultures and traditions. Focus on any image that resides within your sacred circle and use it to inspire your expression of spiritual energy. Or blur the differences between the various traditions and converge them toward the center of the circle. In this midpoint resides the mother ocean for all spiritual tributaries. Drink from this holy water and give it to those who come to you with spiritual thirst. Touch them with the soulful elixir that comes from the fountain of your awakened spirit.

♣

CHAPTER SEVEN

Touched by the Sacred Light

There is no limit to your light, except the dark shadows
of the ego cast upon the sky which we call the self.
Shake your soul! Awaken it from slumber!
The time has come to awaken your divine being.

——PIR VILAYAT INAYAT KHAN

*I*MAGINE YOURSELF TAKING a trip to a nearby city
and on the way feeling compelled to pull the car
over to the side of the road. When you actually pull over, stop the car,
and get out, you walk into the middle of a nearby woods. All this you
do automatically, without any thought or idea about what is happening. In the center of this woods you look up and see an almost blinding light near the top of the trees moving toward you. You are not
frightened, but completely calm and still. You experience the light
bathing you in a warmth and ecstasy unlike anything you have ever
imagined.

When you finally notice that you have been standing in the middle of an unknown woods, you aren't certain how long you have been
there—whether it was hours or days. But you know without a doubt
that the most important experience of your life has occurred and that
you will never be the same. The afterglow of being bathed in that in-

describable light is still with you, and just thinking about the experience intensifies the warmth you carry inside.

As you make your way back to the car, you are struck with the desire to tell everyone in the world about what took place. The deepest part of your being knows that the world would change overnight if you could convey what happened to you in that woods and find a way for others to have the same kind of experience. And then a wave of caution arrives. Slowly you realize how difficult it will be to tell anyone what took place. People might think that you've gone crazy or assume you've gone overboard about some new religion. How will it be possible to say that you feel the most clarity and sanity you have ever known even though you had such an unbelievable experience?

❧ When I was ten years old a revival service was held in my hometown church, and during one of the evening meetings I had my first recognizable spiritual experience. With the church congregation singing the words of "Jesus Is Calling," I felt a mysterious force lift me up and move my feet forward in a church that was filled with a glowing light. In the Baptist tradition, I went to the front of the church and declared that I believed the spirit of Jesus had touched my life. My father subsequently baptized me in a public ritual that confirmed this conversion. I still remember the evening after I was baptized when my grandfather took me on a walk. Near the end of our walk, just outside my house, he stopped, turned toward me and, while looking into my eyes, uttered these words, "You have made the most important decision of your life." That was all he said. Not another word was spoken by him during that walk.

That was the first time in my life that I had encountered a great spiritual force. It was not until college that I had another such encounter, and it was the most unsettling and powerful experience of my life. The month was January and the place was the university town of Columbia, Missouri. It was an unusually warm week, an Indian summer in the midst of what should have been a cold midwestern winter.

While walking along the streets of Columbia, I felt a force take me over. The pervasive feeling was the same spiritual current that touched me as a boy in that late summer revival meeting. As this force or current came upon me, the internal dialogue of my reflective mind became completely stilled. A deep sense of purpose took over the movement of my body, and without consciously directing it I walked inside the university chapel. I will never forget being filled with a very vast sense of awareness. I felt connected to a larger mind and there was an intuition that any question I asked could be resolved by this mind. I walked to the front of this chapel, just as I had walked to the front pew when I was a little boy in my father's country church. I sat down and began feeling the most unusual sensation.

At the bottom of my spine an intense heat began to boil. My insides soon held a fire that burned like the sun. It wasn't long until this fire moved carefully, slowly, and purposely up the entire length of my spine. A tidal wave of fire crept up my body. It extinguished all thought and gave no room for fear. As it climbed up my back, it entered my head and then smoothly flowed out.

When I looked up, I saw that it was now moving as a ball of white light that settled in the front left corner of the chapel. It took the form of a circular screen of light. With tears streaming down my face, I witnessed Jesus as a being of light. He was shown to me as a member of the greater spiritual family that embraced all religions of the world including Buddhism, Hinduism, Taoism, Judaism, Islam, Christianity, and the indigenous spiritual traditions. With open arms and radiating blue eyes, he held a light in his hands that revealed the luminous images of saints, healers, and mystics that had graced these diverse sacred traditions.

I was so taken by this experience that I lost complete awareness of time. I later found out that it took place throughout the course of the night. It was so strong that I had to avoid looking up for several weeks or else the light would start to manifest itself. The light had a voice and a consciousness that now pervaded my own being.

After the experience I was terrified of having it again. I didn't know if I would be able to survive another episode if it were any stronger than the first one. I also didn't tell anyone about it, for fear that they would not understand.

I knew that the experience was a calling to serve others in some spiritual manner. Many years later I learned about spiritual disciplines that were devoted to bringing forth these kinds of engagements with spiritual light. After meeting many spiritual teachers and healers from all over the world, I gradually learned how to bridge my consciousness into the luminous mind that empowers healing and spiritual teaching.

Sacred encounters with light also involve direct transmissions of sacred knowledge. It is a transmitted teaching that radically transforms how you participate in life. It fills you with a trust that there is spiritual guidance and wisdom that is always present.

There is no way to completely convey what the light is like without having experienced it. Louis Armstrong said to someone asking for a definition of jazz, "Man, if you gotta ask, you'll never know." In trying to define poetry, Emily Dickinson wrote, "If I feel physically as if the top of my head were taken off, I know that it is poetry." The light is like that: It takes off the top of your rational head and fully opens your mind and heart. It is the source of all love, the bliss that fulfills every thirst we long to quench. It is the source of all that is spirited, vital, good, and beautiful. The spiritual energy that brings us health and well-being is simply the radiant waves of this light being felt within our bodies.

Near-death experiences and mystical illuminations offer a glimpse of this light. It is the undifferentiated, unspeakable light that is the pure expression of spiritual truth, whereas the specific images and sounds that arise in people's experience are mythopoetic creations that reflect both what the individual brings to the light and what the light brings to them.

People who have come near this light find themselves altered. There is a change in how they relate to death, a new-found sense of eternity, an immersion in the immediacy of experience, and a strong urge to be present in life so as to give rise to soulful, creative expression.

The Divine Light Illumines All Spiritual Traditions

❖ All of the healers, shamans, and indigenous spiritual leaders I have met throughout the world are personally familiar with this sacred light. It initiates them into the spirit world, illumines their holy ceremonies, and guides them to heal others. I have seen the light bathe an entire congregation during a heartfelt prayer meeting of an inner city African-American church, and I have witnessed powerful shamans in the hills of South Dakota and the rainforests of South America actually call it into a ceremonial room.

The Yuwipi ceremony is one of the holiest healing practices of the Sioux. The medicine man is wrapped with a special blanket, bound with rope, and laid upon a bed of sage. The community sits around him facing the altar he has constructed with its mound of holy earth and sacred objects. When the room is darkened and prayers have been sincerely given to the Great Spirit, the drummers and singers cry out for the spirits to come into the room.

Little blue-green lights or sparks the size of fireflies enter the room. They move swiftly, often zooming right past one's face. Sparks also appear when rattles hit the floor, leaving faded streaks of luminescence darting about in the darkness. Once while attending a Yuwipi ceremony held by Gary Holy Bull in South Dakota, I noticed how calm I felt as if some comforting presence was holding my hands. And then I noticed something holding my hands—a pair of large claws! I immediately jumped, surprised by the way my skin had been touched.

These same white or blue-green lights are seen by members of other indigenous spiritual traditions. Among the tent-shakers of the Ojibway Indians of Minnesota and Ontario, Canada, and the Micmac Indians near Nova Scotia, the medicine man enters a tent built for a healing ceremony. When the spirits are called forth, the tent shakes wildly from one side to another and a glowing light shines out of the top.

Ron Geyshick, an Ojibway medicine man, told me about the light he saw during his first time inside a shaking tent. When he entered it, he wasn't sure anything would happen. He had set the tent up on the west shore of the island near where he lives and made a simple prayer that everything would work. As he walked toward the tent, it began to shake. Inside the tent a great wind slapped him around and a whirlwind surrounded his body. He saw little blue and white sparks and watched the tent glow.

Native American Indians have witnessed spiritual light inside the ceremonial place they call a sweat lodge. With a dome made of willow branches and covered with hides, blankets, or canvas to keep it dark inside, hot sacred stones are placed in its center creating an almost unbearable heat. People sit around these sacred stones and pray. I have seen light often appear in the *inipi* or sweat-lodge ceremony, whether as fireflies darting about or as a more cloudlike luminosity appearing at the top of the lodge ceiling.

Throughout North and South America and other parts of the world, spiritual light is present for helping heal the sick. Many of the medicines we use today are known because our scientists collected and studied the plants used by indigenous people. But how did these shamans find the appropriate plants in the first place? Incredible as it may sound, firefly-like lights lead them to the particular plant that will help their patient. These shamans may walk into nature's medicine cabinet and look for a plant that is surrounded by a glowing light. It is the same light seen in sacred ceremonies throughout the world that directs shamans to all the medicines the earth offers for healing.

Vusumazulu Credo Mutwa spoke of his encounters with sacred light. He, too, has seen the nearly blinding light that illumines his culture's spirituality. He also sees people and animals covered with a faint nimbus of light, a halolike light covering them from head to toe. When I first met Credo, his entire head was covered with a cloud of light. I turned to the man who had driven me to the village and asked if he was able to see Credo. He nervously replied, "He's a fog of light!"

These halos and luminous fogs around people, typically referred to as their auras, can be seen by many shamans and healers even with their eyes closed. It is also possible for them to see light that is inside another person's body. Eskimo shamans refer to this as *angakoq,* a view of people's insides where luminous outlines similar to an X ray are seen. This, too, can be seen with open or closed eyes.

Among the Asian traditions are many accounts and highly developed practices for encountering sacred light. When I lived in Japan with Ikuko Osumi, Sen-sei, her entire house became filled with a glowing white light whenever she conducted her healing practice. She, like Credo Mutwa and many other healers, is often seen surrounded by a light.

The Christian tradition is also filled with testimonies about holy light. Jesus was described as a luminous presence, and the angels were often regarded as beings of light. In contemporary times, one of the most remarkable examples of spiritual luminosity takes place every year in the Greek Orthodox celebration of the "Eastern Miracle of the Holy Light of Jerusalem." The Church of the Resurrection that houses the tomb of Jesus is the sight of a recurring spiritual light on the day known as Holy Saturday. At that time a spiritual luminosity often lights the vigil lamp on the holy tomb. Once a guard of the tomb heard the sound of a wind entering the room. He watched a blue light fill the chamber and turn into a tornado that, in turn, became motionless and burst into a great white light. This same holy light also appears to crowds who wait outside the chapel. It may light up or move about as a cloud, disc, or ball of fire.

Wherever you travel in the world, you can find people who have encountered spiritual light. Somewhere in your neighborhood is a housewife, car mechanic, or sales clerk who has seen the light. Take, for instance, the experience of Rosalyn Sutherland, a nurse in Newmarket, Ontario, who entered the hospital room of a sick boy and saw it filled with thousands of rays of light. She never got over seeing that light, and years later she became a healer whose touch sends energy and light to those who are open to receiving it.

Personal Changes Brought about by the Light

✻ All people of the earth are born with all that is needed to have a sacred encounter with light. Before discussing ways in which you can prepare yourself for initiating these experiences, I want to share what is already known about what typically happens when you are touched by the light. Specifically, three personal changes take place: (1) an immediate sense of awakening; (2) an altered attitude about death and dying; and (3) an intense desire for creative expression.

When you read the following ways in which the light may transform you, expect that these changes will occur. What you envision on
a daily basis helps set in motion what will actually take place in your
future.

Outcomes of Encountering the Light
I. AN IMMEDIATE SENSE OF AWAKENING

Imagine looking at the world through a set of binoculars that is never
taken away from your eyes. For weeks you see the world through this
instrument until you forget it is being held in front of you. Then one
day a strong wind knocks the binoculars out of your hands and you suddenly face the world unaided by any mediating contraption. Without
any tubes around your eyes, the world appears to widen, to open up
into a more embracing encounter. Your vision feels naked and more in
direct contact with what you behold. Similarly, spiritual light knocks
away habitually learned ways of seeing and strips you in order to allow
for closer contact with life.

This awakening of the senses allows you to see light where you
did not see it before. You may become aware of halos and auras around
people and luminous fibers that connect you to all other living creatures. This new sight is a quiet and deeply still vision. You see with your
whole body, not through your eyes or through any binoculars, mechanical or conceptual. Similarly, sound covers and moves your whole
being rather than being limited to vibrations within your ears. Your
body becomes the drum upon which the music of the world beats its
rhythms and dances its melodic play. You smell and taste as if you were
swimming in newfound pools of aromatic delight. You feel and touch
the world with hands and body that become electrified by ecstatic fire.

It is through these heightened senses that you are able to heal others. Healers feel their hands have a mind and thirst of their own, wanting to go right to the area of another person's body that needs the

attention of healing touch. When hands touch in this way, they move automatically, directed by energy exchanges that naturally and spontaneously take place.

In this same way, the other person is heard even when they don't speak. They are felt even when they are many miles away. Words are spoken out of your mouth before you have considered talking, and understanding settles upon you before ideas have been articulated within your mind. Spiritual awakenings remove all the barriers that separate you from being in direct contact with the world. They strip and blaze away everything, leaving you so raw and naked that you feel inseparable from the world that beholds and holds you.

A Single Candle

There is a story about a great writing teacher who taught without using a single textbook. All she needed to teach was a candle. For each class she would close the curtains, turn off the overhead lights, and light a single candle. The first time she did this, she told her class, "If you can learn to write about what you see in the light of a single candle, you will help bring forth a great awakening in your life."

And so it came to be that her students would gaze at candlelight during each class. After writing about their experiences, they would share their findings with each other. Some students used great detail in characterizing the flame, noting its shape, movement, and color. Others wrote about what they were unable to see in the flame but were inspired to see with their imagination. For this class, a single candle light became a great teacher.

The students were then told to go to a nearby candle store while pondering this question: "If you believed that the store contained one candle whose light would spiritually awaken you to seeing the Divine Light, which candle would you select?" They were instructed to actually look for such a candle as if they were convinced it was really in the shop. Furthermore, they were to purchase it, take it home, and choose a time when they could be alone with the candle in the dark.

When their candles were completely extinguished, the class gathered all of the paper on which they had recorded the new experiences brought into their life by the candlelight. They took the paper outside to a safe place and ceremoniously lit it with a match, carefully observing the light its fire provided. The teacher reminded them that this was their last day of class. She went on to say that she wanted to leave them with these final words to think about as they silently gazed upon the blazing fire:

"After the candles' lights went out, a new way was opened for bringing another light into the world. One light can truly help awaken another light. Contemplate all the ways light can move from one wick to another. Each lighting and each passing of the flame is a miraculous awakening. As you encounter any light, even the light of a single candle, respect the fact that it may enlighten you and start a great spiritual awakening. And following your awakening, you will help pass the light to others. This is how we keep the light alive."

There is a wick within you that is waiting to become the light of your soul. When this inner flame burns brightly, you will feel a magnificent awakening of your life.

2. CHANGING YOUR ATTITUDE ABOUT DEATH

Ask yourself these questions and take notice of how little we know about the mysteries of life and death: Who really knows which way time's arrow is pointing? Are you now alive and moving toward death or are you moving toward a different birth? Who can prove that you weren't once alive in a different way and through another death moved into this life? Are you now alive in another life you aren't aware of? Could there possibly be many concurrent expressions of your life played out in other dimensions and realities?

Experiences with divine luminosity show existence beyond the physical body and so bring forth many different perspectives on life and death, freeing you to new possibilities for construing the meaning of your existence. Perhaps no insight is as powerful in helping liberate you from the fear of death than the realization of eternity.

The Divine Light embraces all of time. When you behold its luminosity, you brush up against the edge of eternity. You drop the difference separating life and death and immediately experience the greater unity holding you. The light that brings you to the eternal can do more than take you to the other side. It is capable of revealing a place where there is no difference between either side—the sides you now call life and death. In the eternal, you leave the world carved by the knife of time and enter the greater indivisible whole.

3. THE DESIRE FOR CREATIVE EXPRESSION

One of the most dramatic changes an experience of divine luminosity brings is a strong and almost insatiable desire for creative expression, whether it be writing, painting, sculpting, music, cooking, dancing, gardening, or other forms. By participating in creative practices, you feed your newly awakened spirit. Nothing is better for keeping the inner fire of sacred illumination burning than exercising your creative faculties.

The world is filled with theaters, galleries, museums, cinemas, bookstores, forests, playgrounds, restaurants, sports arenas, and so forth that are temples for the practice of creative expression. Revere these places for the spirituality they host. Without the exhilaration that comes from creative expression, our lives would have no soul. Chase the rhythms that move you, give in to the urges to make beauty, and surrender to the desire to please your eyes, ears, and whole being. Sacred encounters with the light help remove the inner obstacles that stand in the way of your searching for ecstatic bliss. The sooner you accept this truth of spirituality, the more easily light will shine on your path of creative expression.

Creativity can be brought into any kind of activity, whether it be writing a letter, working on your car, repairing the screen door, or setting the dinner table. To create is to express life and existence. This is the birthing of soul into our everyday and we should never forget what the early Christian Gnostics knew about spiritual life. For them, and for many other spiritual traditions, the evidence of spirit in a person's life is given by the creative expression they bring into the world. One of their early critics, Bishop Irenaeus, complained that "everyone of them generates something new every day" and that they were bold enough, from his point of view, to attribute their creative experiences to a direct connection with the divine.

A soulful spiritual life is inseparable from a vibrant creative life. To be filled with spirit is to be blissfully intoxicated with creative expression, and to be in the flow of creative process is to open the doors to divine experience.

Encountering the Light

♣ A young seminary student was walking in the snow-drenched woods of northern Minnesota immediately following a blizzard when he saw a light so powerful that it threw him to the ground. He was awakened later by the screeching sound of an eagle whose wing seemed to brush over him.

He ran home to hear his phone ringing. It was a call from his mother, who lived in the hills of Arkansas. Because she was a woman who didn't favor talking about spiritual things, he was greatly surprised to hear her speak of an experience that had just taken place. She was in the woods near a creek when she looked up and saw an eagle flying directly toward her. As it approached her head it stopped and revealed a great light in its eyes. His mother said to him, "Son, I looked into the eyes of God." Both mother and son were shaken by the two events that occurred at the same time in their lives. It led the young man to find out more about his grandfather, his mother's father, a man who had been an Indian medicine man closely allied with the eagle and the land underneath its outstretched wings.

You do not have to be in the wilderness to be touched by the light. It may come to you while you're shopping. A university student of mine was in a local bookstore when she opened a book and felt currents of energy go down her body. Everything she read in the book was experienced as if she were literally drinking the written words. In the midst of the bookstore, a light appeared and engulfed her. Without knowing what was happening, she experienced a luminous energy come upon her that changed the course of her life.

Sometimes the sacred encounter with light is simple, though no less powerful. A woman I know was playing with her daughter when she looked up and saw light emanating from her own child's face. Moved to tears, she was overcome with a love and understanding that she had never known before.

The light has been seen as a luminous cloud, a magnificent flying disc, a thin, laserlike beam, an array of blue-green dots that dart about like fireflies, or as a huge circle of beams that completely engulfs a space. The light may be felt rather than seen. It may be experienced as a great luminous warmth, covering you with new insight and guidance.

The teaching of illumination was regarded by Walt Whitman as "the knowledge that passes all the argument of the earth." It is a teaching that takes place through the absorption of light, as the great mystic Evelyn Underhill described it. In these experiences, the pure light of the divine streams into your soul. This inner illumination enables you to see things as they are. You begin seeing the interconnectedness, relatedness, and eternity that holds all of life.

Gautama Buddha declared that the "noble truths" he taught were not "among the doctrines handed down," but that "there arose within him the eye to perceive them, the knowledge of their nature, the understanding of their cause, the wisdom that lights the true path, and the light that expels darkness." Our truest teachers are those who bring down the light so that it may powerfully ignite the wick you carry in the center of your soul.

EXERCISE ONE

A Sincere Request for Illumination

✣ Faithfully ask for spiritual guidance and illumination and carry this request with you throughout each day. Anything you can do to remind yourself of this request will help keep you tuned and oriented toward bringing forth the light.

On a small piece of gold paper, write these words: "I am open to receiving the Divine Light." Sign your whole name below this statement and fold the paper once. Carry this folded paper with you throughout the day and frequently open it and read the declaration. Remember to fold it again so that you will have many opportunities for opening it throughout the rest of the day.

After doing this for a week make another declaration, this time writing these words: "I am opening myself more to receiving the Divine Light."

As before, sign it, fold it, carry it with you, and open it throughout the day. After a week of carrying this declaration, make a third one with these words: "Please show me how to become more prepared for receiving the light."

Carry this message with you until you think of another declaration you can make for yourself. When one comes, write it down and maintain the practice of opening these declarations throughout each day. Continue this practice as a way of preparing yourself for an encounter with Divine Light.

As part of your sincere request for illumination it is also important for you to develop a willingness to sacrifice something important. This may mean your career, financial security, professional reputation, grade-point average, popularity, friends, and so forth. This willingness does not necessarily mean that you will actually sacrifice these things but requires that you develop the belief that you would do so if necessary. Recall the classic story of Abraham, who was asked by God to sacrifice his own son. With great grief he obeyed God and brought his son to the sacrificial altar. In his willingness to make the greatest sacrifice a parent can imagine, God spared his son's life.

To receive the light you must temper your will and become more available to be moved into the Divine Light. Do not forget that all spiritual traditions ask you to sacrifice yourself in order to become part of a greater spiritual life.

At the beginning of each week, choose one small thing that you will sacrifice for that week. You could give up having desserts, drive your car less, sleep less, carry less money, use one particular word less, use less water for domestic tasks, carry less stuff to work, comb your hair less, worry less, complain less, judge less, look at your watch less, touch the refrigerator door less, read the newspaper less, or give less time to watching television. Allow these small weekly sacrifices to convince you that you are capable of making a larger sacrifice if called upon to do so.

EXERCISE TWO

Preparing a Place for the Light

♣ In seeking the sacred light, I find it useful to find or set up a place that is totally in the dark, the same setup used for many traditional ceremonies. Not a single ray of outside light should be able to penetrate this space. The place of absolute darkness can be a room, a closet, or a private corner in your basement or attic, or even an outside tent or natural cavern.

Either alone or with friends, place yourself in this darkness and sincerely ask out loud for spirit to come and present itself as a Divine Light. Try to avoid doing this with someone who brings doubt or insincerity to the occasion. They may affect the ability of others to sufficiently open themselves. When you are able to gather a small group of sincere seekers, the power of bringing forth light is usually amplified.

It helps to have an attitude that holds two simultaneous and somewhat contradictory intentions. You should deeply and sincerely desire that light appear, while at the same time you should have no expectation for any particular outcome. If you balance these two intentions, you will move into a midplace where a quieter seeing may take place. Such a state of mind never asks the question of whether you are seeing light. It is more of a state of complete presence and absorption into the moment.

When you first see the light, do not fall back into the ordinary habits of mind that examine, evaluate, explain, and study it. This may extinguish it. Do not attach yourself to the light in any particular way. Simply behold it and allow it to embrace you.

Making a Link to the Creative Force

❧ Connecting yourself in some way to the creative force provides a conduit for receiving spiritual light. Acts of creative expression are always rooted to the spirit. It is this thread of connection that provides an opening for spiritual light to enter.

What forms of creative expression speak most deeply to you? Whatever your response, immediately start searching for it whether it be music, visual images, food, conversation, theater, overhauling your car, sewing a new outfit, or any experience that brings you great bliss. The best place to start is to simply follow the trail where you hear the call of ecstasy. If you are taken to the heavens by a certain kind of music, then by all means bring this music into your life. Keep it present throughout your daily living and follow where it beckons.

Throw yourself into any project that really gets your creative juices flowing. Become obsessed with this project and pretend that it is the most important part of your life. As you open the door to creative expression, remind yourself that this is a way of building a tunnel to the light that can transform you. Every step forward in a creative project carries you closer to the light.

If you have trouble thinking of a project, here is one you can consider. Begin by getting yourself a portable tape recorder. Carry it with you into a library and go to the section of books that you find most meaningful. Gather a stack of books that appeal to you and seek a private place in the library with them. Randomly open up each book and whisper the first paragraph you find into the microphone of the tape recorder. After you have done this with each book, go home and listen to the words you spoke. Listen to them every night and begin appreciating that you have made a vocal collage. Identify the one sentence in this collage that is most powerful for you. On a large canvas or piece of paper use a paint brush to write this sentence.

Live with this painted sentence for one week and then place it on the floor. During each day for the next two weeks, look for some small object that you believe is related or connected to the sentence. It may be a tree branch or some small item you purchase or anything that is meaningful to how you understand the sentence. Bring one such object home every day and attach or glue it to the sentence on the spot you believe is most appropriate. When your work of art is complete show it to several friends you think would be respectful of your creation. Ask them to observe it but not discuss it. Request that they give you one word that best conveys the meaning of the work you created. Collect some special words in this way. Write these words onto your work and consider them the signature of the piece. But continue to work on it if you feel inspired.

What you choose to do in a creative work is less important than losing yourself in the project. Getting out of your own way helps open a door to the flow of creative energy and serves as a conduit for encounters with the sacred light.

EXERCISE FOUR

Imagining the Light That Weds You to Others

✣ Create the image of a great soft and calm light engulfing your whole being this very moment. Imagine it is there even if you can't see it. See another person entering the room where you are now sitting and saying to you, "My heavens, what is that light that surrounds you?"

You trust this person and you ask them to give you more details about what they see. In this conversation, the two of you discover that the color and intensity of the light surrounding you changes with the feelings you have for the other person. When you open your heart to the holiness and integrity of the other person's life, the light grows brighter.

Imagine inside your mind's eye that you begin seeing a light around the other person who is observing you. It, too, changes its color and intensity as their feelings shift about you. See the two of you becoming so captivated by watching each other's light that you stop talking and just concentrate on shifting your feelings in a way that intensifies the light. You now have such strong feelings that you can no longer experience any difference between seeing the light and feeling something about the other person.

At this moment a pronounced swooshing sound is heard and you feel the floor drop open. You fall into a blinding light that combines all of your sensory processes into a new kind of experience. All of your senses—touch, taste, sight, hearing, and smell—are transformed into being raw, crackling energy. As it crackles like beautifully contained lightning, see it turn into a solid glow of powerful light.

Observe this light return all of your senses to you, one by one. Now each sense has been bathed and cleansed by the light. You are able to see more clearly than you ever had before and hear more intensely than was ever before imaginable. You can smell and taste what you see and feel what you hear. A new world of experience has been created and blessed for you through this initiation into holy light.

Think of this particular guided journey into your imagination every evening before you go to sleep. Start keeping a diary next to your bed. Do not record your dreams in this book. Instead, write down the sacred encounters with light you hope you will have in your dreams.

Do this before retiring into the dark every single evening for the rest of your life.

Reaching the Sun

✛ In a very special place next to a gentle stream, there once lived a worm covered in a cocoon. In its sleep it dreamed of becoming a creature with wings that would someday fly toward the light. One day the worm transformed into a most beautiful golden butterfly. Immediately it started flying toward the source of light it had seen in its dreams. And then it heard the voice of an eight-year-old girl.

"Butterfly," she asked, "where are you going?" "Why, I'm going to the light," the butterfly responded. She explained how there was no need to go to the sun when all you had to do was look around and see how the whole world was lit with golden rays of sunlight. She talked so long that it started to get dark outside. The impending darkness worried the butterfly and it began to nervously shake its wings. "What's happening to the light?" the butterfly finally blurted out.

"Don't worry," the girl answered with a smile. "It's only the sun blinking its eyes." She then explained how it's daylight when the sun opens its eyes and evening when the sun's eyes close.

Our butterfly soon fell asleep and in its dreams it flew all the way to the sun and asked the sun why it had to blink. The sun started laughing and the butterfly woke up. He rushed to share his dream with his friend, but she was asleep on the grass.

Within a moment or two, the butterfly was completely overtaken by the realization that it was only when his eyes were closed that he could dream of safely flying to the sun. At that moment, he thought he heard the low, rumbling voice of the sun utter an almost inaudible whisper of thunder, "Yes, I close my eyes so I can dream of seeing your light."

It may not surprise you to know that the butterfly became very confused. He could no longer bear to be alone with his quandery, so he flew over to the girl and landed on her ear, tickling it so she would be awakened. After telling her everything he asked, "What do you think it all means?"

As the girl spoke, the butterfly began seeing a beautiful golden circle all around her. As this circle began to glow with more and more light, the butterfly found he was unable to listen to her in the way he had listened to her before. His heart was becoming very full with the beauty he saw around and in her, and it was touching him in a way he knew must be the feeling people referred to as love. The light he saw around the girl not only grew brighter, but it also grew larger until it began encircling his own body, wings and all. When fully illuminated, the butterfly shouted out, "I see! I see for the first time!"

The girl stopped talking and looked at the butterfly and saw it engulfed by a circle of beautiful golden light. She did not know that the light she saw came from her own light, in the same way that the butterfly didn't see that his light was what was surrounding the little girl. She exclaimed, "I see, too! Thank you for teaching me about the light."

At that moment, the sun, who had been observing and listening to what was taking place, smiled and winked. In the darkness of that wink the girl and the butterfly flew together right into the center of the sun.

CHAPTER EIGHT

☙

The Passion of Soul: Moving from Self-Esteem to the Spiritual Stream

I saw myself on the central mountain of the world,
the highest place, and I had a vision because I was seeing
in the sacred manner of the world. . . .
The central mountain is everywhere.

—BLACK ELK, LAKOTA SIOUX

D URING HIS CHILDHOOD, my son developed a restlessness that threatened his ability to sleep. After weeks of worrying about him I received a fax from Japan. A translator had sent a message from Osumi, Sen-sei. She believed my son was on the verge of becoming sick and that it was important that I immediately make preparations for him to be healed. I was absolutely stunned by how she could know what was going on. I had not communicated with her, and she was thousands of miles away.

That night, to my even greater surprise, my son called me into his room and asked me to do something special to help him get to sleep. I tried singing by his bedside with all that my heart could give until I collapsed next to him with exhaustion.

My right hand then spontaneously touched the top of his head and my left hand covered his heart. Within seconds my head and hand began to vibrate at a very high frequency as if I had been plugged into some kind of mysterious electrical current. My son immediately went to sleep and his body jolted several times from what I assume was a transmitted current. As I wondered whether this energy would heal him, a great calm suddenly descended upon us. A warm and powerful light entered my body and went directly into his.

As we receive the light, we become moved to bring it into others. As we help it come to others, the light quenches our own thirst for spirit. A respect for collaboration and cooperation overtakes the more limited desire of self-actualization or individuation and we develop a clearer sense of how helping others is the purest and surest way to help ourselves. When we serve others it is not enough to do it in order to earn spiritual brownie points. Spirituality suggests that we see the other as if we were viewing ourself. This being in the other's mind and realizing them as part of our mind precipitates an opening of our compassionate heart. The more our mind is moved into the world in this way, the more it readies itself as a spiritual vessel.

Life in the Spiritual Stream

❧ The spiritual stream has its tides and currents that move up and down. The moment we find peace and calm, life slaps us with another challenge, whether it be the sickness of our child, an impasse with our boss, an increasing personal debt, a leak in the roof, or a noisy neighbor. I know people whose lives are so filled with distress that the only respite they get is attending their weekly church services. This is particularly true for the inner-city church. Some of these parishioners have more trouble and woes, living in a street culture of violence and poverty, than most of us would be able to believe. Yet some of them find a great peace and calm through a spiritual practice that enables them to walk through their lives by holding on to each Wednesday night prayer meeting and Sunday morning service. It would be a true crisis if a single service were ever cancelled.

For many Native American Indians, their church is the sweat lodge, a simple structure that is filled with sacred, steaming rocks for around a dozen people to enter and pray. When they "go sweat," there is a cycle of breathing that organizes the ritual. Each time the door is closed, the heat aims to bring each person to the limit of what they can bear. You sometimes feel like you could die in that heat, and the appropriate passage through a difficult sweat is to give up worrying about your comfort (and survival) and turn to praying for your relations and environment. After each person has given their prayers, the sweat lodge door is opened, allowing fresh air to enter. This cycle is repeated four times, into the dark heat of the lodge and then into the refreshing breeze from the outside.

A spiritual miracle takes place when you use prayer to move your focus away from personal discomfort. You give up worrying about yourself and give into trusting spirit. When this takes place, the interior dark of the sweat lodge begins to be filled with light, and the uncomfortable heat transforms itself into the healing breath of spirit.

Our life in the spiritual stream is not one of constant illumination and ecstasy. It moves back and forth like the movements of breathing, taking us into the light and expelling us from it, over and over again. In the tides of the spiritual stream we learn more fully how light and dark are inseparable. We reach a deeper calm about how life brings us suffering as well as joy and that the two contrary experiences are as naturally joined as inhaling and exhaling the air we breathe.

Our mission as spiritual beings is to be at ease rather than disease with the natural movements of life, accepting what comes to us as grist for the next movement. In suffering, we prepare for grace and in that grace we are made more ready to learn from suffering. This grace is the free, unconditional love that flows from the Divine. Our task is to move our suffering away from the shadow of despair and place it under the light of grace.

For many years my father struggled with alcoholism. The uncertainty that surrounded his life often made it difficult for me to get close to him. Every hope for his recovery would be followed by a heart-breaking disappointment. Without knowing it at the time, I began to emotionally distance myself from him. Even after he had gone through treatment and made a new life for himself, our distance was still present, not articulated, but silently felt.

One day my father called saying that he had been diagnosed with ALS, or "Lou Gehrig's disease," and that he might not be around for long. His body was beginning to deteriorate and he had to give up his job. At the time I didn't know whether to believe him, wondering whether he was drinking again and that his condition involved alcoholism. To my horror he kept getting worse until he could barely walk.

I had a dream one night that I was with my father. In the dream I went up to him and touched his neck with my right hand. When I did so a torrent of pain filled my neck and body, causing me to shout out in agony. This awakened my wife and after I told her about the dream, I noticed I could not move my neck. It felt like the whiplash I had once received from a car accident. It took a week to recover from the pain and loss of mobility brought by the dream.

I knew I had to make a trip to see my father and to meet him with open arms. I told him about the dream and asked him if I could put my hands on his neck. With tears flowing down each of our faces, I felt my whole head vibrating at a high frequency while heat flowed out of my hands. Even my father asked whether I was alright due to the amount of heat he was feeling. We felt the presence of his father in the room. In this moment of completely opened hearts, spirit healed the distance that had come between us.

I knew then that I must take him to the Mayo Clinic. Within weeks he saw their neurologists, who diagnosed his condition as extremely severe spinal decompression caused by stenosis or bone spurs on the vertebrae of his neck—it was the same spot I had experienced in my dream and felt moved to touch. He underwent surgery and, following a week where he could not move, the doctors lifted him out of bed and helped him take eight steps. The surgeon, Dr. Meyer, said to him, "The surgery has saved your life. Now let's get you back home again."

The pain and suffering of my father led to a healing in our relationship and helped bring our family back together again. As he learns to walk and begin a new life, I know that I will always be there for him and will never stop being grateful for the sacrifice his pain made for our healing.

Perhaps the pinnacle realization of life in the spiritual stream is how we may trust ourselves to the webs of relationship that hold us. As we trust relationship, we are brought more deeply into spirit. Here breath is again found—a moving back and forth between the rhythms of separateness and connectedness. As unenlightened individuals we enter into the sacred relationship to be reborn as individuals inseparable from relationship. The recycling of life through reproduction, breath, relationship, and spirit constitutes the breathing of soul.

No matter what spiritual tradition you are part of, the ascents and descents of a soulful journey will always bring you back to the beginning center point of stillness and a don't know mind. There the strongest medicine ever known to anyone, love, will break your heart and open your mind to be reborn to the hope-giving realization that we receive all that we need when we give all that we have. Those are all the operating instructions we need to turn on our soul.

Waiting with Dadirri

❧ The Aboriginal word *dadirri* refers to the quiet and still awareness that arises from the deep spiritual spring that is within every person. To the Australian Aborigines, healing, guidance, and peace come from visiting this place within. You may be taken there by walking alone in the bush, taking part in a ceremony, or by simply being quiet. In our place of stillness, we learn to be patient and wait for spirit. Through this waiting we make ourselves available to be swept into the rhythms and time of spirit rather than the hustle and bustle of our artificially wound up clocks.

Waiting is valued by Aborigines as a spiritual practice, as a way of being still without impatience or boredom. They wait because they know that spirit is already here and that its presence is a love that is gentle, tender, patient and kind. Dadirri reminds us that waiting is the companion to stillness. They are the two sides of the emptiness or don't know mind that makes us available to being touched by spirit. Spirit waits for us in dadirri, the deep, quiet spring whose waters are so still that a single idea or the smallest act may stir up a tidal wave of change. This spring is found within our heart, and its tributaries move life throughout our body. There all wisdom resides. It is the home for our soul and a spiritual outpost and oasis for others who have lost their way.

The exercises in this book require an attitude of dadirri for them to be most effective in helping you breathe soul into your everyday life. Do them with a stilling of your expectations for any particular timetable for change. Be at ease with your life experiments and practices, allowing them to join you with the rhythms of soul, but doing so in their own time.

In the quiet of spiritual calm you become tuned, analogous to a piano string being tuned, so that the music of life may be played more beautifully upon and through you. When we move our lives to becoming more finely tuned instruments, we are more easily moved by the rhythms and vibrations of spirit. The call of soulful spirituality stops us from trying to quench our deepest thirst by getting full of something, whether it be romantic love, financial success, drugs, power, knowledge, spirit guides, secret understanding, or self-esteem. Soul is about getting in tune so that you can more easily move with the rhythms and vibrations of life.

Ram Dass, a respected spiritual teacher of our time, took a pilgrimage to meet his teacher in India and ask him for guidance. Maharaji replied: "Be like Christ, Christ died for your love." Ram Dass was caught off guard by this answer. He was a Jew who had gone to a Hindu temple in India to be told about the New Testament. When Maharaji was asked how to meditate like Christ, he closed his eyes and wept and then said, "He lost himself in the ocean of love." When he was asked how to awaken inner spiritual energy, he replied, "Serve everybody." And when he was asked how to know God, he answered, "Love everyone."

When we enter the divine stillness and simplicity of love, all is well. It requires, in the words of T. S. Eliot:

A condition of complete simplicity
(costing not less than everything).
And all shall be well . . .

No matter how clearly it is stated or how poetically it is expressed, many of us can't believe that the quenching of our deepest thirst can be done by simply getting ourselves in tune and in rhythm with the soul of life. We still think that all prizes must be earned or achieved or bestowed upon us. Our education has so effectively engrained within us the ideas of competition and success that it is practically unbelievable for us to imagine that the most important answer lies in our stopping all the fuss and being in tune and falling into the rhythm now.

The Art of Heart and Beauty

❧ The Jewish theologian Martin Buber once said, "All suffering prepares the soul for vision." Hemingway, in *A Farewell to Arms,* wrote that "life breaks us all, and afterward many are strong at the broken places." Oscar Wilde recognized that it is our brokenness that opens us to spirit: "How else but through a broken heart can the good Lord enter in?"

We never know how spirit will deliver its force, whether it will work through a teacher's gesture, tone of voice, glance, or silence, or whether it will be through the way life breaks us. But whether accompanied by the cry of a pummeled heart or the hope of a long-awaited sojourner, when the spirit comes it blows the ego-centered mind, dashes our logical expectations, and touches us in a way that is beyond measure.

Spirit not only touches us when we are broken but may do so when we don't expect it. A friend of mine once asked Mother Meera, an Indian avatar who is said to be an incarnation of the Maha Shakti, to bless her mala, a strand of prayer beads. Mother Meera smiled and reached for them, quickly tossed them into her other hand, and tossed them back. While the beads were in midair, my friend thought to herself, "That's it? Those beads couldn't have been blessed." She felt cheated. The minute the beads landed in her hand, though, she felt the most exquisite energy run up her arm, into her heart, and throughout her whole body.

The spiritual traditions that have developed a deep awareness of the complementarity of opposites, such as the Navajo and the Tibetan Buddhist, practice a paradoxical relationship to the contraries of life. They acknowledge that bliss and suffering are two sides of the same coin and are therefore the same. This kind of double viewing helps one develop a respect for both sides of all distinctions. When we do harm to harm, then we also are doing harm to what is good. This realization must be maintained, respected, and revered as a way of keeping spiritually balanced and in tune with the natural spiritual order. This is the path to beauty and to the stillness that enables beauty to be realized in everyday life.

There is no better place to begin our soulful walk into beauty than to move away from the temptation to judge. There is no sacred purpose served in discerning who is evil and who is good, who is enlightened and who is not, or who is in and who is out. Every human being is nothing more and nothing less than fully human.

This ultimately means we are as evil and as good as anything that can be imagined. We each are capable of the most horrible sins and the highest acts of good. There was once a great Teton Sioux medicine man who regarded himself as "lower than any condemned man anywhere." This is true for each of us in that we have committed every crime, if not in public, then in the unspoken darkness of our imagination.

Soulful spirituality is not about finding where we are and then moving toward where we think we should be. It necessarily includes a dying over and over again so that we may be continuously reborn into the center of self-lessness. It takes the time to find the right container for our practice, changing the form until we feel at ease and have complete trust in it. We must also find the open arms of a heart ready to embrace and balance all contraries, oppositions, and difference. Holding the world in this way releases our attachment to any particular part of it and enables us to enter the greater mind, breathe the deepest breath, and feel the most moving soul.

There was once a monk alive during the time of Buddha who everyone thought was stupid and lazy. His brother was his abbot and became so fed up with the monk's inability to learn or do anything correctly that he beat him up and threw him out of the monastery. The monk wandered around until another abbot took pity on him, but the same thing happened. Everyone got fed up with his stupidity, beat him up, and kicked him out. Finally, he met the Buddha who took him in and gave him only one task—no studying, no meditating. He was to sweep the meditation hall every morning saying to himself, "Clear the dust, clean the dirt." He was fully enlightened within the year. No one else in any of the other monasteries was close to his stage of development. We do not learn or evolve in straight lines.

Begin ambiguating, lubricating, and loosening the distinctions that separate the holy from the profane, the enlightened from the lost, the teacher from the student, and the healer from the one healed. The earth and the sky must dance together and our bodies must soulfully move with our imagination. Our life must be given back to nature so that we may receive the truest nature of our being.

The Zen Buddhist D. T. Suzuki commented that the real world includes both horseflies and champagne and that one is as good as the other to a person who has fully realized the nature of reality.

The Divine Play of Co-Presence

You speak like a person who would pronounce half of the notes of the scale—say, do, re, and mi—to be sacred, but fa, sol, la and ti to be only profane, while, Madam, no one of the notes is sacred in itself, and it is the music, which can be made of them, which is alone divine. If your garter be sanctified by my feeble old hand, so is my hand by your fine silk garter. The lion lies in wait for the antelope at the ford, and the antelope is sanctified by the lion, as the lion by the antelope, for the play of the Lord is divine. Not the bishop, or the knight, or the powerful castle is sacred in itself, but the game of chess is a noble game, and therein the knight is sanctified by the bishop, as the bishop by the queen. Neither would it be an advantage if the bishop were ambitious to acquire the higher virtues of the queen, or the castle, those of the bishop. So are we sanctified when the hand of the Lord moves us to where he wants us to be. Here he may be about to play a fine game with us, and in that game I shall be sanctified by you, as you by any of us.

—ISAK DINESEN

✣ Hinduism speaks of a well-known image of a "net of gems" where in every gem of the net all the other gems are reflected. When life is seen as a "net of gems," it becomes impossible to suggest that any part is separate from its whole. We can not say that the nose our finger points to is exclusively a "part" of our body. Our nose is a part of our body, but it is also our body. Seeing others is not only a way of seeing a part of our interaction with them, it is also seeing our whole relationship with them. In the fullest view, parts and wholes are not one, not two. There is a necessary complementarity that returns us time and time again to realizing the necessity for the co-presence of both part and whole, life and death, success and failure, health and pathology.

When we join with the divine play, daily life is lived as a ceremony. Like the Navajo, we may choose to sing blessings throughout the course of every day, repeating words like, "In beauty we dwell. In beauty we walk . . . The beauty is restored. The beauty is restored." However far we have to roam and no matter how many foreign doors we enter, we must eventually come home to find the beauty in the shrine

that we call home. There we will enter the divine play of the everyday
and be blessed with beauty and soul.

The Final Letter: Learning from Death

☙ Imagine that you have passed on from this life and now are in the
world of spirit. There you are given the wisdom of the universe. You
learn how some of the ideas, rules, guidelines, and practices that are accepted on earth are completely erroneous. You are also shown that some
of the most important spiritual truths and practices aren't even known
by most religious traditions. And finally, you are baptized in a sacred
pool that brings forth pure luminosity, crazy wisdom, energy, vision,
and creative expression, forever changing everything that you believe
and desire.

To celebrate your initiation into the other side, you are given one
more opportunity to have a moment of direct contact with the human
species. You may contact those that you love the most, whether it be
your daughter, son, spouse, parent, partner, or friend. You may do this
by writing them a letter telling them anything you have learned from
the other side. Consider what you will say and how you will say it. Pass
on what you believe is most essential regarding life in the spiritual
stream.

Now actually write this letter. Take as much time as you need and
allow yourself as many rewrites as necessary until you feel it is right.
When the final letter is completed, mail it to yourself. After it arrives,
read it as if someone who cared for you had written it. Place this letter
in a special private place and wonder what would happen if you believed
and followed its advice. Consider allowing one week of the year, perhaps around the time of your birthday, to be a special occasion for the

letter to be revisited and revised. Annually mail the ever-changing letter of advice to yourself and ceremonially dedicate yourself to bringing its wisdom into the world.

EXERCISE TWO

From Impersonation to Evolving Your Own Style: How to Follow the Tracks of Others and Still Find Your Own Soul

✣ It is important that you find your own style of spirituality. Sometimes the best way to begin involves following the tracks of someone else. For example, a student of jazz may seriously study the recording of a song played by another musician whose work deeply moves them. They will listen to the song hundreds of times, until every note is committed to memory and can be played in the same way as the original performer. After doing this to a few tunes, they find that they can absorb the other person's style of playing.

The next stage of learning involves tinkering, varying, and improvising off the memorized musical arrangements, until a unique way of playing comes forth that utilizes the natural resources the performer brings to the music. This is how they give birth to their own style.

With a similar strategy, Benjamin Franklin learned to write by copying the *Spectator* papers written by Addison and Steele. After he copied an essay, he would set it aside and try to rewrite it from memory. He would then check to see how accurate his reconstructed paper was, and study all the mistakes he had made until he was able to write a perfect copy. After several months of this practice, he was able to move away from imitating his mentors and create his own style of writing.

Find the spiritual words, phrases, ceremonies, and practices that speak to your heart and start using them on a daily basis. Use these as a stepping stone for developing your own style. Appreciate how we stand upon the inspired works of others in order to find our own voice. Life in the spiritual stream is not only a recycling of yourself, but a recycling of the contributions of others into your whole being. Recycle the spiritual offerings and gifts of others and then pass them on. In this way, the spiritual stream constantly flows throughout the community.

EXERCISE THREE

Allowing Life to Make You Happen

✤ There was a legendary teacher of piano in Boston named Madame Chaloff. She taught Keith Jarrett, Herbie Hancock, and other revered musicians of our time. What made her unique was her mystical approach to creating an effortless performance of music.

She claimed that the secret to playing music involved learning to play one note perfectly and effortlessly. She taught one basic lesson: how to play completely without effort. Musicians were often shocked when she told them to spontaneously produce only one note. In the beginning, they were often limited to only practicing five minutes a day. With time they moved into more effortless playing, until they discovered how to let the music naturally play itself rather than working to make it happen.

Spend some time living effortlessly, even if it's only five minutes a week. Examine your life and find what it is that you do that is natural, effortless, and spontaneous. It could be anything: walking, fishing, reading, or cooking. Whatever it is, bring more of this effortless living into your week.

Begin with at least one minute where you exert no effort or purpose to an aspect of your life that is presently taking too much work. Build up this time and believe that it is possible to live each day with less effort. Move toward having a day where you find that you simply happen.

From time to time there will be interruptions and stumblings about. Being in the groove is also a rhythm, and you will fall out of it so that you may later fall back into it. This rhythm is no different than any other pattern within your life. We breathe back and forth into all that we are.

EXERCISE FOUR

Being a Gentle Spirit

✴ Spiritual power does not flex any muscles or display pride. Its strength is found in the moments when we are gentle with one another. We appreciate how fragile our condition truly is and we gain a new respect for the temporariness of all our relationships. When you are with your child and fully realize that the particular moment will never be repeated again, you are drawn into a more sacred and gentle presence.

Gentleness values the softly spoken word, the tender touch, the warm embrace, and the kind, approving gesture. When we are in the presence of holy people, it is the power of their gentleness that moves us the most. Their quiet way of being deeply present with others outweighs all of the words of wisdom they may speak and all the cleverness, creativity, and magic that may take place around them. It is their consideration of others that brings forth their fullest presence.

The world needs more gentlewomen and gentlemen. Practice being more gentle in all that you do. Begin the practice of gently stroking the palm of each hand with your fingertips when you wake up in the morning and when you retire in the evening. Do this as lightly, calmly, and gently as you can. See your life as residing in between these rituals of gentleness that take place each morning and evening. If you need more kindness in the course of your day, find a way to gently stroke your palms again. This will help introduce gentleness into your consciousness.

Proceed to exercise some act of kindness that is gentle. Be nice in a more gentle fashion, whether it involves kind words, actions, thoughts, or feelings. And be more gentle with your own life, bringing more softness, quietness, tenderness, and consideration to it. It is gentleness that makes us lighter, enabling us to more easily move into the quiet place of spiritual presence.

No Goal

♣ The exercises in this book are all about helping you open your don't know mind, breathe the soulful rhythms of stillness and energy, make gentle grace out of everyday life, find the bliss in your heart, trip yourself into truth, dream yourself into the Dreaming, ride in the direction spirit is going, and passionately embrace the light. Rather than follow a regimented procedure for doing these exercises, let your own attraction to an exercise be the guide to choosing which one to work with. Consider opening the book as performing a divination. Continue doing so until you find an exercise that seems to be "calling" for your practice.

These exercises give you an idea of the kind of practices that are useful in awakening the spirit in everyday life. Feel free to make any alteration of a practice, and encourage yourself to dream up new ones. Rolling Thunder, a Cherokee and Shoshone medicine man, used to say that you should take a look at how others bring spirit into their lives. Then it's important to work out your own songs, your own methods, your own prayers, and the things that go with it. John Fire Lame Deer, the great Sioux medicine man, reminds us that "medicine men—the herb healers as well as our holy men—all have their own personal ways of acting according to their visions. The Great Spirit wants us to be different." In this spirit, I invite you to use the exercises in this book as a way of tripping yourself into finding your own way. They have been useful to me and to others in finding our own way and were born out of the greater crucible that includes the spiritual practices of all the traditions of the world.

Each of us must eventually find ourselves coming home to the place where we trust our heart to be most open and compassionate. I am grateful to all the spiritual elders and teachers who have helped lead me home.

Over and over again, every road I follow brings me back to the light. There I find the only miracle that is worth living for—the miracle of illuminating love. There are many seductions and distractions along the spiritual path, but the true road is paved with loving light. Trust nothing but the light, and open your heart with complete trust when it shines upon you. Embrace the daily moments that cultivate your awakening. Smile and bestow grace upon others, knowing that the gods smile with you.

There has never been anything for you to acquire, know, or conquer in order to enter the kingdom of light. All that is required is your trust in life and the fullest awareness that you are meant to be illumined by all that has blessed every enlightened being throughout the whole of time. Open your eyes and behold your awakening.

APPENDIX:

☙

Overview of Exercises

INTRODUCTION

1. What do you believe in?

Imagine being in an airplane that is about to crash. What spiritual source would you call out to?

I. PREPARING THE GROUND

Chapter One. The Unquenchable Thirst

EXERCISES:

1. Acknowledging the Thirst: Inviting Spirituality into Your Life

Write a letter inviting your chosen form of spirit into your life.

2. Undermining the Desire to Understand

Turn "why" questions into "how" questions as a means of encouraging yourself to participate in life more fully. Participation in daily life, not a retreat from it, is what leads to spirit.

3. The Return to Stillness: Being Present Rather than Reactive

Get a clicker toy to use every time you react without thinking. Explore your subconscious for a device such as a sound or an action to cut through reactivity.

4. Letting In Love

Choose three days in which you behave toward a loved one as though these were the last three days you will spend together.

Chapter Two. Making Grace out of Life's Disturbances

EXERCISES:

1. A Past Fast

Spend time each day living as though you've forgotten who you are and where you came from, in order to loosen the grip of the past.

2. Starting Off Small

Set small goals for making positive spiritual changes.

3. Recycling Yourself

The five-minute, end-of-the-day detox meditation on light.

4. Hatching Your Bliss

Write what your greatest bliss would be on a piece of paper and place it under your mattress at the level of your heart, in order to begin working it into your dreams and later your conscious mind.

Chapter Three. Tripping Your Self: The Spirited Performance of Crazy Wisdom

EXERCISES:

1. Using Nonsense to Help Free You from Over-Understanding

Begin to develop don't know mind by creating a certificate that reminds you to let go of intellectual control.

2. Fooling Around with Your Least Important Routines

Nurture don't know mind by performing routine tasks as though they were sacred acts.

3. Have a Dinner Conversation Where No One Tells the Truth

A tool for uncovering your deepest truths. The fiction often tells the real story.

4. Spiritual First-Aid Kit: Antidotes for Closed Minds

Put together an emergency kit to be used when you feel blocked. It could contain a small feather, a miniature toy animal, and a collection of humorous quotations.

II. LIFELINES TO SPIRIT

Chapter Four. Being in Rhythm: The Opening of the Heart

EXERCISES:

1. Finding the Rhythm of Your Breath

While watching your breathing, begin to listen for the rhythm that makes you unique.

2. Carrying Rhythm into the Everyday

Remembering to feel the rhythm of every activity and interaction.

3. Seeing with Your Heart

Let go of judgment by remembering that everyone is alike in not wanting suffering and wanting to be happy.

4. Opening the Hearts of Others

Showing enthusiasm for others' efforts and achievements in our daily relationships helps open our own heart as well as others'.

Chapter Five. The Dreaming: Entering the Light of the Night

EXERCISES:

1. Daydreaming about Night Dreaming

During the day, set aside time to imagine what a meaningful dream might be like. Draw a picture of that vision, reproduce it, reducing it to the size of a stamp. Place the image inside your pillow.

2. Catching a Dream

Place a net or other object by your bed at night, creating a ritual in which a spiritual dream is asked for.

3. Stimulating Your Unconscious with a Bedtime Story

Use the stories in this book, or other stories, to activate the unconscious before sleep in order to bring forth a dream with spiritual content.

4. Tying a Cord to Spirit

Learn to access the mystical dream body by tying a physical cord to an image of it before going to sleep.

III. LIVING WITH MYSTERY

Chapter Six. Awakening the Spirit: The Reception and Nurturance of Vital Life Force

EXERCISES:

1. Milking the Source: The Rocking Exercise

Set aside time each day to sit on a bench or chair and allow your body to begin its own natural rocking motion. This is an ancient exercise for activating the life energy that opens us to feeling spiritual presence.

2. Improvisational Touch

Learn to allow the hands to be taken over by their own natural healing knowledge by working with someone close to you.

3. Dancing in the Dark

Learn to dance your own rhythm in order to open to spirit.

4. The Sacred Circle of Healing

Make a sacred circle, or mandala, from the healing traditions throughout the world into which you invite spirit.

Chapter Seven. Touched by the Sacred Light

EXERCISES:

1. A Sincere Request for Illumination

Write a series of notes to yourself with sincere messages expressing your desire to see and experience the light of spirit.

2. Preparing a Place for the Light

Create a sacred space in which you await your encounter.

3. Making a Link to the Creative Force

Bring into your daily life a new act of creativity. This is also the force of spirit.

4. Imagining the Light That Weds You to Others

Meditation on the light that surrounds yourself and others.

Chapter Eight. The Passion of Soul: Moving from Self-Esteem to the Spiritual Stream

EXERCISES:

1. The Final Letter: Learning from Death

Imagine that you have already left the earth, and from this new perspective write a letter to a loved one about what you have discovered. Mail it to yourself once a year.

2. From Impersonation to Evolving Your Own Style: How to Follow the Tracks of Others and Still Find Your Own Soul

Begin collecting words, images, music, practices from spiritual traditions and practitioners which strike a cord for you. From this, you can begin to develop your own brand of spiritual practice.

3. Allowing Life to Make You Happen

For one minute each day, focus on effortless living.

4. Being a Gentle Spirit

Introduce an act of kindness and gentleness into your everyday life.